A Treasure
We Call Home

A Treasure
We Call Home

RICK CRARY

Cover photo by Rick Crary

Cover design by Michelle Leurie Burney

Treasure coin images on cover courtesy
Florida Division of Historical Resources

Indian River Magazine – *A treasure to read*

To Publishers Gregory Enns and Allen Osteen, I extend my special thanks. *Indian River Magazine* generously granted me the right to republish any of my articles, which previously appeared in that publication and in *Fort Pierce Magazine*. I selected ten of those stories to include in this book with minor revisions, including changes to some of the titles.

CONTENTS

Illustrations and Credits

Acknowledgments

So many people have provided me with valuable information and encouragement. First, I would like to recognize historian Sandra Thurlow, whose books contain a wealth of information about our region. Without her prompting, I'm sure I never would have started on my project of rediscovering local history. After Sandy persuaded me to give a history talk about Crary House at City Hall in 2010, Pat Williams and Adrienne Moore spurred me to go on Janie Gould's *Floridays* radio show to discuss research I had undertaken concerning Governor Martin. It was Janie who first suggested I write something for *Indian River Magazine.* Publisher/editor Gregory Enns allowed me generous space in his magazine where most of the stories in this book appeared. Mark Tomasik, Editor of *Scripps Treasure Coast Newspapers,* granted me free rein in his archives and gave me many encouraging comments. Historian Joe Crankshaw took me under his wing when he recruited me to participate in the *Stuart News'* centennial project. Historian Alice Luckhardt shared valuable research with me. Jo and Ron Paradise kindly allowed me to rummage through their private collection of documents and photographs. Harry Quatraro, Registrar of the St. Lucie County Historical Museum, opened up the archives at his disposal and tracked down some of the items I needed. Mary Jones shared useful resources on hand at Stuart Heritage Museum. Jennifer Esler and her staff at the Elliott Museum shared materials retained by the Historical Society of Martin County. Kathleen Garrett Roberts aided me with genealogical research. Peggy McCarty Monohan placed her family records at my disposal. Dr. Jerald T. Milanich, Curator Emeritus at the Florida Museum of Natural History took time to answer several questions. Eminent historian Dr. Eugene Lyon shared some of his valuable research with me. Donna Crary and Gwen Carden each proofed my final manuscript and offered valuable advice on punctuation; but to the extent I neglected to follow it, any mistakes are my own. Michelle Burney designed the book's cover and straightened up my layout. Oh, and there are many others to thank, especially Denny Hudson. Over coffee downtown on multiple occasions, he provided the perfect audience for me to present the intended plots of most of my stories. And when he found them highly entertaining, I would go home and write them down.

For Donna, Ricky, and Christopher.

When color goes home into the eyes,
And lights that shine are shut again,
With dancing girls and sweet birds' cries
Behind the gateways of the brain;
And that no-place which gave them birth, shall close
The rainbow and the rose.

Still may time hold some golden space
Where I'll unpack that scented store
Of song and flower and sky and face,
And count, and touch, and turn them o'er,
Musing upon them; as a mother, who
Has watched her children all the rich day through,
Sits, quiet-handed, in the fading light,
When children sleep, ere night.

The Treasure,
— by Rupert Brooke, 1914

The Treasure

It's still out there beneath the waves, beneath the sand—the gold that spilled from Spanish ships and named our Treasure Coast. It's still out there—our history buried by heedlessness and time. The wood of forests that made majestic fleets, the hand-woven sails decorated with painted crosses—they've long since washed away with lives of people poured by storms into a hostile sea. The swirl of tides and churning waters push and pull the years away. And centuries bring great kingdoms down—and civilizations. But the gold is there, and the silver pieces of eight. You have to look to find them.

This collection of historical tales is part of my own personal treasure hunt. I have always been a history buff, but only recently did I challenge myself to view aspects of our broader American history from the vantage point of the place where I grew up. The story of a community—any community—is interwoven with the history of all mankind. Every venue can be a place that summons riddles, timeless truths, and hidden meanings. Why not draw the threads together from somewhere close at hand? After more than half a century on Florida's Treasure Coast, I finally began to revisit the past to see what I could piece together.

So much has disappeared. We Floridians allow the sandcastles of our history to wash away as quickly as tides roll in. We are forever racing onward toward the *new*. Like a Ponzi scheme, our boom-based economy demands a steady influx of newcomers. We drain away fresh water and flood the land with people whose common factor is displacement. Too few recall where Florida has been.

The Treasure Coast seems especially new. It is a place of many beginnings, but none of them took hold until after a sundered nation forced itself back together with a Civil War and Reconstruction. Three hundred years of Spanish occupation left no lasting landmarks, nor did the British interlude. A colony established along the Indian River in the 1840s failed. Forts of palm logs on the shore were abandoned and soon decayed. By the 1860s the region returned to a state of nature mirroring the dawn of time.

While most of the country was busy welding itself into a bustling morass of industrial might, our forgotten swamps and lowland jungles became the nation's last frontier, where wildlife reigned unchallenged.

If you had ventured down the Indian River in 1879 with Dr. James A. Henshall, a famous sport fisherman of that day, you would have found our skies filled with the whooshing wings of thousands of ducks. Roseate spoonbills and prehistoric-looking pelicans owned Atlantic breezes. Waters of the rivers and the sound were clogged with long sea grasses teeming with fat tarpon, black bass, and manatees.

That was the era when a new set of dreamers taught themselves how to tame the land. Pineapples and the Homestead Act joined forces to awaken visions of riches in this faraway subtropical realm. Anyone, except for former Rebels, could get free land from the federal government if he staked out a claim and farmed it for five years. Handfuls of hardy pioneers came to our shores. Most of them had foreign accents: German, British, Scandinavian. Throughout the 1880s, they shipped small stores of their produce north by boat, and their settlements remained primitive and remote.

Henry Flagler's railroad connected the region to the rest of the world in 1894, because he needed to reach his new hotels down in Palm Beach and Miami. Pineapple lands on the Treasure Coast were only an afterthought for the man who owned the tracks, but his railway made plantations boom. Some of the pioneer planters traded shacks in for mansions, but their time of riches was short-lived. As soon as the mighty Flagler got into the pineapple game with his Cuban competition, he was bound to win. The budding communities of the region slid back toward a state of nature once again.

Then the land gambling of the Roaring Twenties ensued. Florida's politicians conspired with the homefolks to use sunshine to lure away the bulging wealth of the country's industrial states. Tens of thousands of Northerners hopped into their Tin Lizzies and rode down to boomtowns like Miami and West Palm Beach to speculate on the soaring value of sand in paradise. Property was subdivided into as many tiny lots as possible.

Would-be entrepreneurs on the Treasure Coast wanted in on the action, too. That's why they persuaded a new young governor to pare down Palm Beach and St. Lucie counties to create new counties called Indian River and Martin. But they came to the table much too late. The poker game was ending, and the great land boom went bust.

All over Florida, newly planted communities went to seed. The hamlets and little towns of the Treasure Coast were financially ploughed under, too. For decades they would languish in a state of slow decay. One local newspaper claimed the sound of a hammer was not heard in the area for many years.

In 1927, 22-year-old Evans Crary, my grandfather, was one of the few newcomers who moved to Stuart not long after Martin County was created. Within three years he was elected as Stuart's municipal judge. Within a decade he became the county's state representative to Tallahassee. In yet another decade, he became Speaker of the Florida House of Representatives, and then state senator. He beat rivals who had been here longer, and the family he founded stayed on. Today, in comparison with so many other newcomers, our ties seem ancient. But ironically, I first saw this place through the eyes of a newcomer, too.

Although I was a third-generation resident of Martin County and had lived here for my first two years of life, I didn't remember anything about the place when we moved back in 1961. By then I was six years old. In the interim, we had lived in Washington, D.C., Mexico City, and Gainesville, Florida. In comparison with world capitals and a bustling college town, Stuart seemed to me like a quiet place at the far end of the world. It was mostly made up of scrubby woods and water. The major advantage of moving here for me was that I was allowed to play in the street. In Gainesville I had not been permitted to tread beyond the curb in front of our apartment building. Traffic was so sparse in Stuart, I could ride my bike anywhere I wanted without much danger of getting run over. My little dog, Rebel, always tagged along.

In St. Lucie Estates, which borders the wide St. Lucie River and narrow Krueger Creek, there were few houses and many vacant lots with plenty of grapefruit trees. I didn't realize the subdivision had been one big plantation of pineapples, grapefruit, and mangoes until about 30 years before I was born. In season, the fruit ripened in abundance. A dozen or more of us boys from surrounding neighborhoods would sometimes gather for grapefruit wars. The fruit made an excellent, cannonball-sized weapon, which was far superior to the dirt clods we tossed at each other in the Broadway Section on the other side of East Ocean Boulevard. The bright yellow missiles were fun to dodge, but a fresh grapefruit could knock the wind out of you. A sour splash from a rotten one drew fruit flies, which tickled your face relentlessly until the battle was done.

Many decades later I learned how prominently St. Lucie Estates had figured in the formation of Martin County and how the dashed dreams of its developers resulted in so many lots remaining vacant for more than 40 years. The great Florida land boom of the 1920s must have lit up the sky like a million bottle rockets all being shot off at once. The darkness of the bust that followed seemed to last forever. But it was only a change of tide.

After the City of Stuart cut my grandparents' home in two and relocated it downtown where it was reassembled, Sandra Thurlow, one of the county's premier historians, asked me to give a talk about the history of that house. I had saved old letters and some of my grandfather's legislative papers, which I found in the attic when I was younger. Many years before, I had also interviewed my late grandmother and typed the transcripts. With additional research gathered from old newspapers, I had plenty of threads with which to weave an emblem of county and family history using the house as my central prop. I wrote the essay *Crary House* to hand out when I gave my talk.

That first encounter with the local past awakened a curiosity for other things I wondered about when I was very young. I turned my explorations into stories, and Gregory Enns, the publisher/editor at *Indian River*, put most of them in his magazine. Janie Gould interviewed me several times on her WQCS radio show, *Floridays*, and one of the episodes was broadcast statewide on Public Radio. Those successes encouraged me to keep searching for more strands from long ago. The result is the tapestry of tales I have woven together in this book.

As a child I was fascinated with presidential history. To impress adults and kids, I often spouted out trivia about the occupants of the White House. Denny Hudson, the present CEO of Seacoast National Bank, was one of my best friends. One time he did me one better by boasting that his grandparents possessed one of Grover Cleveland's oars. I didn't believe him, of course, and I demanded immediate proof. We hopped on our bicycles and rode over to his grandparents' house on the river to rummage through their garage. Denny had to summon his grandmother to come out and verify that the oar he showed me had, in fact, once belonged to the former president.

"Yes," Mrs. Hudson assured me. "President Cleveland used to fish here many years ago."

Well, I couldn't believe that either. Why would a president ever come to tiny Stuart, Florida? There was nothing here but mosquitoes and sand flies. Decades later in *Our Accidental Tourist*, I finally admitted the Hudsons' assertions were true. We were not quite as cut off from world history as I once imagined.

Denny and I divided a large paper route between us, and we covered for each other when needed. The newspaper only came out twice a week at that time. On Wednesdays and Saturdays we picked up our newspapers at the *Stuart News* building, which used to stand across from the courthouse on East Ocean Boulevard. I had three baskets on my bicycle, and with 250 papers stuffed into them it was hard pedaling, especially against a stiff subtropical breeze.

While I was rolling my pile of newspapers and securing them with rubber bands, I sometimes saw a haggard man hunched over an old-fashioned typewriter. He usually had a cigar in his mouth that hid his uncertain smile. Although my mother told me Ernie Lyons was a special person, I couldn't see it then. It was only when I researched *The Timeless Voice of Ernest Lyons* that I realized what a philosopher and true man of letters he really was. I had not expected such greatness could have come from my little hometown. As I drew closer to the words he left behind, my appreciation for the natural beauty of our region also grew tenfold.

Another story I never quite believed while growing up was that Hobe Sound was once on the verge of becoming the motion picture capital of the world. The place was all sugar sand and sandspurs to me, so the tale seemed too farfetched to give it credence. I never liked being fooled. Was the story true or just another big illusion like the movies gave us? When I wrote *The Lost Magic of Picture City* I was astounded to find just how close the legendary Selznicks came to making that pipe dream a reality.

Even as a child I had a vague understanding that Henry Flagler had some connection with our area. His name has long been impressed on one of our streets in downtown Stuart, where the little railway station used to stand in front of the historic Lyric Theatre. I loved the railroad Flagler built. We still had passenger service when I was small, and my mother and I took the train up the coast. But it wasn't until I met my future wife in Jacksonville that I began learning more about the man who played both a productive and a destructive role in Treasure Coast history.

While I was dating Donna, we made many day trips from her home to St. Augustine, where Flagler's first palatial hotel still stands. It is Flagler College now. On Christmas Eve in 1982, we got engaged in the beautiful Memorial Presbyterian Church that Flagler built to the memory of his daughter, who died in childbirth. Flagler was laid to rest beside her in 1913. I chose that famous cathedral as the place to give Donna a diamond ring, because we had gone there the first weekend we began dating in 1979. It is one of those rare places in Florida which has not been scathed by time. In a way, I feel I owe a debt to Flagler for opening the state to my ancestors and for providing a landmark that reckons prominently in my own personal history. I searched for the shadow the titan cast on the Treasure Coast, when I wrote about his influence in *Lord of the East Coast of Florida*.

For as long as I've been going to the beach, I have always loved watching pelicans dive into the ocean. Until I researched my story about Pelican Island, I never realized how close they once came to extinction. When I first began to drive—an old 1967 Volkswagen—the former Lyons and Crary bridges were drawbridges. I never minded getting caught when a bridge went up. I would get out of my car and gaze at the gliding pelicans. Probably I wished I could soar away with them. So many years later when I wrote *The Pelican Precedent*, I felt I had discovered kindred spirits in Frank Chapman, Paul Kroegel and Theodore Roosevelt, who are featured prominently in that tale.

Although Governor John W. Martin blessed my county with his name and created Indian River County, too, most of his fingerprints have been wiped off the pages of Florida history. I spent one of my vacations trying to rescue him from the list of time's missing persons. I found the area where he was born north of Ocala in Marion County, and I visited the villages where he went to school. I located the boarded up building that once housed his law office on Adams Street in Jacksonville and the yellow brick mansion he built on the St. Johns River in Avondale. In Tallahassee I stood in his former hunting lodge, and I walked a hall of the Old Capitol that once led to his office. One morning I spent a contemplative hour beside his grave in Jacksonville.

The most striking illustration of just how far Governor Martin has fallen into obscurity came when I visited the State Archives at the Capitol complex. I had called ahead to make sure they had some of his papers, and a volunteer told me they had one small box. But when I made the long trip up to Tallahassee, the clerks all said they had nothing. I insisted someone assured me they did. They looked and looked and finally found it. A clerk told me Martin's box had been unmarked until then, and she thought I must have been the first member of the public ever to have asked to see it. In *Florida's Great Gatsby Governor*, I have tried to make Martin less of a stranger to his people.

I wrote *A Tale of Two Judges* in response to a request from Gregory Enns, who wanted a story for *Fort Pierce Magazine* about a famous trial that took place in that town. When I was a little boy, my grandmother told me all about the dreadful Chillingworth murders. I remembered the harrowing details of that horrifying crime. She and my grandfather had been social friends of Judge and Mrs. Chillingworth, and Chillingworth's father had been Palm City's first developer. Coincidentally, the week before Gregory requested the story, I bought a copy of Jim Bishop's old book, which contains raw transcripts of Judge Peel's murder trial. I found it at O. Brisky's bookstore in Micanopy, while I was hot on the trail of Governor Martin.

My grandfather was a political ally of Governor Dan McCarty, and in the early 1980s I worked on a congressional campaign with the governor's son, the late Mike McCarty. So, it was with great interest that I researched the life and shocking assassination of the founder of the McCarty dynasty: Charles T. McCarty. While writing *Death of the Pineapple King*, I gained a clearer understanding of how the Treasure Coast was advancing toward prominence during the pineapple boom. McCarty's untimely death meant the region lost the only man who might have had sufficient stature and political pull to stand up to Flagler, when he turned on the local pineapple growers and busted their boom.

As a lifelong Civil War buff, one of my early disappointments growing up in Stuart was learning that the Union and Confederacy never contested Constitutional issues in our region. Besides some incidental blockade runners seeking brief harbor in local waters, the biggest connection our area had with that terrible war was when Confederate Secretary of War John C. Breckinridge fled down the Indian River with Yankees in pursuit. I retraced his escape route in *The Vice President Who Became a Pirate*. The story also gives us a glimpse of just how wild and uninhabited the Treasure Coast was when most of America was already a bustling industrial empire.

When I began researching *Discovery of the Treasure Coast*, I was hoping to prove Ponce de León might have stopped here to pick up water or firewood on his way back down from landing in St. Augustine. I did my best to uncover the location of the stone cross he used to mark one of our rivers. I never expected to find a credible argument that the great explorer might have actually discovered Florida around Vero Beach. That story was my unabashed effort to join in the 500-year celebration of Florida's discovery in 2013. It was a lot of fun to write. I also got a real eye opener as to how seemingly solid history is sometimes built on very flimsy foundations.

In *Our Titanic History* I set off on an all-absorbing journey to rediscover the vast sweep of Spanish colonial history and how it touched our Treasure Coast. The Spaniards held onto Florida much longer than we English-speaking people have, and yet we have retained so little of their experience on this ever-changing stage. That's part of the mystery of our fabulous peninsula, I suppose.

One of my most recent adventures in time travel took me back to the heartland of Florida that I never intended to leave behind. When I was a child, my grandparents owned 40 acres on the South Fork River next to a ranch. They had two small, rustic cottages there. I spent many endless weekends and vacations out in the back country traipsing through the wilderness alone. On Adams Ranch, legendary rancher Bud Adams has wonderfully preserved vital aspects of Old

Florida that I thought had long since disappeared. In *The Majesty of Cattle Country*, I've tried to preserve them, too.

Lastly, it is the prerogative of writers of self-published books to celebrate history that comes closest to the heart. In *Old Times There Are Not Forgotten* I have added a tribute I wrote to my late grandmother. More than anyone else in my life, Talley McKewn Crary taught me how to experience the sense and feel of days gone by. And in *Savoring the Journey*, I pay tribute to my wife, and offer a glimpse of how history intertwines itself into our daily lives.

History filters through us all, whether we recognize it or not. At some point in life you realize the treasure chest of time you've been given is running out of moments, and the best way to replenish it is to think on what's been spent. Reclaiming the past is not a fruitless exercise in nostalgia; it is a way of enhancing an understanding of our link in the chain of time. It is a way of recovering a *sense of place* in this land of ceaseless change. It is a way of returning to find what I think all of us are really looking for in the end: a treasure we call home.

Our Accidental Tourist

Former President Cleveland on one of his fishing trips in Stuart.

In those days the waters ran clear. We can only imagine the beauty and color of the St. Lucie River reflecting in Grover Cleveland's eyes. The first time he saw it was in 1900, some 15 years before soldiers started digging the canal to Lake Okeechobee, which would muddy the cast of the river forever. A cornucopia of aquatic life teeming in the broad expanse between the river's distant banks is something we must find in our mind's eye. It drew the ex-president of the United States to return to our shores time and time again.

When the 63-year-old Cleveland discovered Stuart, it was the latter period of the town's pioneer days and the final years of his life. Much about the area had changed already, since the first inhabitants settled some 18 years before. Hubert Bessey and his brother, Willis, first sailed up to the point where the forks turn north and south in 1882. The Bessey brothers veered south and picked a spread of land to clear. Ernest and Otto Stypmann followed on their heels, as did other mostly

German and English immigrants. Soon vast swaths of thickets and woods disappeared under budding pineapple fields.

After the railroad came in 1894, a hamlet took shape around a ramshackle line of buildings near the tracks. That's where Stuart's residents congregated for social reassurance. A few of them were present when Grover Cleveland emerged from his private railway car. The ex-president was surprised to see their village, and the locals must have been flabbergasted to see him, too.

History has its happy accidents. Cleveland found Stuart by mistake. It was the sort of thing that can happen in the dark. Who was responsible? We do not know. During the night someone mistakenly decoupled the ex-president's railway car and left it stranded in Stuart as the locomotive pulling his train chugged onward to Cleveland's intended destination. He was probably on his way to Palm Beach, where some friends vacationed. Until he woke up in the morning, he didn't notice that his private car had stopped clacking down the tracks. The rotund ex-president with the famously hefty moustache lumbered off on gouty feet in search of a telegraph office. It wasn't far away.

Cleveland, who had left the nation's highest office only several years before, couldn't have been happy about being abandoned at a hole-in-the-wall stop. But folks lingering around the post office made him feel at home so quickly that he decided not to wire an SOS to the railroad office. The two-time president, who presided over a span of the Gilded Age, felt suddenly charmed by Stuart's rusticity and its river. Perhaps the German immigrants reminded him of old chums in the beer halls of Buffalo, where he spent so much time in his younger days. Or maybe he was persuaded by the long-bearded postmaster, Broster Kitching, whose kind and gentle English manners made him a favorite around the village.

Stuart's railroad depot in pioneer days.

Incredibly, the political superstar chose to stay and try the fishing in tiny Stuart—and he returned for many more winters. To realize just how amazing that must have seemed to villagers, you need to know that rich and famous people of that day spent their winters luxuriating in Henry Flagler's palatial hotels in Palm Beach and Miami. They had electricity down there, and indoor plumbing, and ballrooms, and an army of servants to pamper them—and every convenience and delicacy known to the era was made available. Why, they even had ice cream!

Stuart had none of that. It had outhouses, and oil lamps, canned goods, and pine knot fires, and no fresh milk. The well water wasn't cold, and the bathwater wasn't hot. Ice was shipped in on the train, but it melted so fast that only people living near the station could get it home in time to store it in their crude ice boxes. There were no automobiles, no real roads, just cumbersome wagon trails. Most people boated to and from wherever they had to go. How could a man who was used to having his own newfangled telephone in the White House, not to mention all the elegance afforded by the nation's highest office, be happy in a place that must have been less glamorous than Hooterville?

Well, for one thing, Grover Cleveland loved to fish, and the St. Lucie River had the best black bass fishing in America. Dr. James Alexander Henshall said so. Henshall was the famous sportsman who authored that stirring best seller from the 1880s, *The Book of the Black Bass*. But the part about the St. Lucie River having the best fishing in the country was written in Henshall's other book: *Camping and Cruising in Florida*. That book didn't sell as well, but the locals probably cited it for authority when they made arguments as to why the former president should kick up his heels and stay.

Cleveland could have fished in Lake Worth or Biscayne Bay and vacationed in the luxury to which his former prominence in world history should have accustomed him. When President Grant retired, he took a much-heralded trip around the world with his wife, Julia. Dignitaries celebrated and entertained the Grants like the American royalty they were in country after country. But Cleveland just wanted to fish and hunt ducks in Florida. And though he probably had reservations to lodge at one of Flagler's big hotels, he really didn't care for pomp and circumstance. Rich food upset his bulky stomach. His tastes were simple, his manners plain.

Believe it or not, Cleveland didn't like living in the White House. During his first administration as the 22nd president, he bought a nearby farm, where he preferred to stay. The press dubbed the place "Red Top" because of the color he painted the roof of his farm house. Cleveland and his young wife, Frances, tried to limit their nights at the White House to months during Washington's two social seasons, when custom demanded their presence. He sold their farm for a handsome profit after he lost the 1888 election, but when voters returned him to office as the 24th president four years later, he rented another house in Washington called "Woodley."

An article appearing in the November 9, 1906, edition of the *St. Lucie County Tribune* captured the essence of why Cleveland instantly fell in love with Stuart: "Some years ago, when Mr. Cleveland first came to the East Coast to fish, he came to Stuart and wished to be recognized as a common citizen, who came to fish and not be interviewed, to be on exhibition, to be used as advertisement, and the people of Stuart have respected his wishes. H.W. Bessey, of Stuart [Stuart's first settler], has always taken Mr. Cleveland and his party out on their fishing trips." In Stuart, the former Chief Executive—so weary of the public stage—could discard all the pretenses that burden the powerful and be himself. He was a common man at heart.

Cleveland had experienced perhaps the most meteoric rise to the top in American political history. He came from nowhere: his family was poor; he never went to college; from an early age he had to work. Eventually he clerked in a law office and passed the Bar without formal training. By 1881, he was just a 44-year-old bachelor practicing law in Buffalo. No one outside that city on Lake Erie had heard of him. Three years later he would win the 1884 Presidential election and head off to Washington to run the country. What! How did that happen? People later explained it as "Cleveland luck." We might also call it an extreme case of "being in the right place at the right time."

It almost sounds like a fairy tale. The nation was thoroughly sick of a slew of corrupt politicians. The 1880s seemed particularly shady. Year after year, everywhere you looked you discovered your leaders were on the take. Graft was the rule of the day. Bosses of Tammany Hall, and robber barons, and so many other bad guys had politicians dancing on strings like the money-hungry marionettes so many of them were. Was there no man in America who couldn't be bribed?

Well, in 1882 Grover Cleveland became the mayor of Buffalo, and the first thing he did was veto all the phony city improvement contracts that padded politicos' pockets. Reporters were happily astounded. News spread across the state of New York about a rare sighting of an unusual species: an honest politician. Without even meeting Cleveland, the head of New York's Democratic Party announced he had discovered his party's winning gubernatorial candidate. The voters agreed. In 1883, Cleveland moved into the governor's mansion in Albany by himself—he was still a bachelor. He continued to root out corruption, and suddenly the entire country heard the story of "Grover the Good." Of course they wanted to make him president.

A few weeks into his campaign for the presidency, the Republican opposition dug up a dirty little secret to tarnish Cleveland's knight-in-shining-armor reputation. Back in the 1870s, Cleveland fathered a child out of wedlock with a loose, hard-drinking widow named Maria Halpin. At least, he could have been the father, and he knew it. They didn't have paternity tests in those days.

As you can imagine, campaign officials were horrified. "What are we supposed to say now?" one of them asked in desperation. From his besieged mansion in Albany, Governor Cleveland sent a famous three-word telegram that saved the campaign for righteousness and won him a term in the White House. The telegram he sent back to his supporters said: "TELL THE TRUTH."

Supporters were much relieved. He's still "Grover the Good" after all. Even when he screws up, he doesn't run and hide. He always tells the truth, just like young George Washington. That was the party line.

Well, the Republicans were having none of that. They continued to snipe at their opponent, trying to get as much mileage as they could out of Cleveland's sex scandal. No doubt you've heard their famous slogan:

> *Ma, Ma, where's my Pa?*
> *Gone to the White House—ha, ha, ha!*

James G. Blaine, the Republican candidate, was no saint either. He got caught writing letters that made it look like he might be expecting to receive graft. The 1884 election was remembered by some historians as the dirtiest in American history, which is saying something, because we've had a bunch of dirty ones. Cleveland came out on top and his supporters came up with a counter-slogan to celebrate their triumph:

> *Hooray for Maria! Hooray for the kid!*
> *I voted for Cleveland, and I'm damned glad I did!*

Cleveland wasn't the paper-doll president his party's bosses hoped he was going to be. They couldn't clothe him any way they wanted to. He had a mind of his own, and he always believed his own opinions were the right ones. That's how he got his nickname "Grover the Obstinate." People started turning his virtue into a liability, calling him "ugly honest." His terms in office were mostly stormy, but he and his 21-year-old bride, Frances Folsom, got plenty of good press when they held their wedding ceremony in the Blue Room of the White House.

In 1897, when Cleveland left office after his second presidency, he was as one newspaper called him, "one of the best-hated men in the country." He had presided over a depression called the Panic of 1893, for which he was given blame. He was a vocal anti-imperialist in a time when his countrymen were itching to extend Manifest Destiny across the globe. Many were upset when he tried to give the Hawaiian Islands back to Queen Liliuokalani, because he thought his predecessor had stolen them. Congress wouldn't let him. He angered agrarians by making their debts heavier under the gold standard than they would have been under "free silver" inflation. And although he scolded Wall Street's monopolists for their selfishness and greed, he refused to support effective governmental controls to curb their practices. He alienated everyone! At his last State of the Union Message, only four people were said to have clapped. No wonder his reception in the Stuart Post Office warmed his ailing heart.

In those days Stuart was in Dade County, which stretched from the southern banks of the St. Lucie all the way down to where Miami-Dade County is now. According to the Federal Census of 1900, that vast chunk of land had barely 5,000 inhabitants. Most were living in the burgeoning settlements growing up around Flagler's mighty hotels. Stuart was so remote and so sparsely populated it must have seemed like the perfect place for a wounded fisherman-president to hide.

He came down again and again, sometimes with notable friends like Joe Jefferson, a famous actor of that day. He usually stayed three to six weeks and enjoyed the accommodations at the Danforth Hotel, which was managed by Hubert Bessey and his wife, Susan. On March 28, 1902, the *Times-Union* in Jacksonville reported that the former president and his wife passed through the city on their way to Stuart "...where Mr. Cleveland goes especially to take advantage of the fine fishing facilities there." A follow-up story in the *New York Times* on April 12th said his wife left for home by herself after two weeks. The next year on February 9, 1903, the *Times* said that he was in Stuart again, fishing for tarpon in the St. Lucie River. Another story mentioned he also went fishing on the nearby Indian River. On March 4th the newspaper reported on his return to Princeton, New Jersey after several happy weeks in Stuart.

"We had a very enjoyable time down in Florida," Grover Cleveland said, "and we spent a considerable part of the time boating and fishing....I am feeling very well and am sure that the trip has benefited me very much."

In 1905, the *Ocala Evening Star* reported on yet another sojourn in Stuart, as did the *New York Times*, which characterized the Stuart area as "the swamps." One newspaper mentioned that Cleveland's friends were trying to get him to try the fishing down in Palm Beach, but quite obviously, he was stuck on Stuart. After half-a-dozen annual fishing trips, he decided to make his stays more permanent. On April 6, 1906, the *St. Lucie County Tribune* reported the following:

CLEVELAND TO BUILD
A HOME IN STUART

Lately it has been learned that ex-President Grover Cleveland, who for many winters has been coming south to Stuart, in the northern part of Dade County, has purchased a plot of land in the town and will erect a substantial winter home thereon. The seller was Ernest Stypmann and the deed will be recorded in Miami within the next few days, says the Tropical Sun.

All the world knows that Grover Cleveland is an enthusiastic fisherman and all the world knows also that Florida is his favorite stamping ground.

That was the year Cleveland celebrated his 69th birthday on March 18 at the Danforth Hotel, which stood high on the river bank next to where Shepard's Park is now. The parcel of land he bought for himself was where City Hall stands today. That year, his wife stayed home with their children in Princeton, where they had chosen to settle after leaving Washington.

The day after his birthday, he wrote a letter to his 10-year-old daughter Marion, whom he called "Mimsie." He told her how unbelievably warm the March weather was in Stuart. Why, it was nearly eleven o'clock at night, and he was sitting in his hotel room with no coat on and all the windows open! But he did mention that he didn't know if his little girl would like the place. There wasn't much to do besides fishing and swimming, and the sport fishing might be too challenging for her—not like the easy catches they made back home. What he meant was the fish in Florida were very large and they were real fighters. His letter said he and Professor McClanahan of Princeton had caught thirty "big heavy fellows" that day.

Mimsie Cleveland could have played with Josephine Kitching (later Josephine Taylor) if she'd ever been allowed to come down. Josephine was a little girl who lived down the street from the Danforth Hotel. Decades later she fondly remembered sometimes watching the former president. She would see him sitting in a boat drifting in front of her house. In her handwritten memoirs, she recalled him being a "great fisherman." She remembered Mrs. Cleveland coming to Stuart to spend part of her husband's winter vacations with him. Mrs. Cleveland took many walks by herself along the river in front of her house and through her yard. One time Josephine was invited to join the Clevelands down at the Danforth Hotel's dock, where she tired herself out entertaining the famous couple with all the diving and swimming tricks she could do. The Victorian house where she resided with her parents, Walter and Emma Kitching, still stands on Atlanta Avenue today.

During Cleveland's 69th birthday vacation in Stuart, the *New York Times* reported the nation's only living ex-president caught one of the biggest tarpons ever taken in Florida. By then America was warming up to its discarded leader again. Two years later in March 1908, *Appleton's Magazine* described a happy ending to Cleveland's rise-and-fall experience: "It isn't often given to a man to live through a rise Napoleonic in its swiftness to jump to the highest place in the nation; then, with blighting suddenness, to find himself a shattered idol with few to raise a friendly voice against the storm of denunciation, and finally to see that same nation come back to greet him in humble friendliness." That same month the *Panama City Pilot* added: "The public attitude toward Mr. Cleveland has changed until he is now fairly deserving of the title given him last year as 'the most distinguished private citizen in the world.'"

In 1907, Cleveland wrote a small book to express why he loved communing with nature so much. In his *Fishing and Shooting Sketches* he said, "In this domain, removed from the haunts of men and far away from the noise and dust of their turmoil and strife, the fishing that can fully delight the heart of the true fisherman is found; and here in its enjoyment, those who fish are led, consciously or unconsciously, to a quiet but distinct recognition of a power greater than man's, and a goodness far above human standards."

Cleveland's health was failing, and it wasn't just his usual attacks of gout. He suffered from a persistent intestinal ailment, and his kidneys were shutting down. His heart was weak, too. As he was dying at his home in Princeton, he must have realized he would not live to build his dream winter home, but he longed to see Stuart one more time. He wrote a letter to Hubert Bessey, asking him to reserve two rooms at the Danforth Hotel for himself and a private nurse, but the trip never transpired. Grover Cleveland could barely sit up in bed. The

19

New York Times reported that his family was trying to help him get over missing his usual Florida vacation. He lingered through the rest of winter and spring and breathed his last in June of 1908, reportedly saying with his dying breath: "I have tried so hard to do right."

This is the tale that should not be forgotten by the people of the Treasure Coast: A famous leader—a truly honest, incorruptible man—rose and fell and rose and fell again in two completely separate presidencies. And when most of his countrymen shunned him and turned away, seemingly forever, a few people in a faraway rustic hamlet called Stuart made him feel entirely accepted and at home. He was just an accidental tourist, and they took him in. They gave him a hideaway once a year, a place where he could be himself and heal during his darkest days. Stuart and its peaceful river sank into his soul. And in the end, the fallen leader was recognized as a great man once again, and he died amid the applause of a nation he had tried so hard to set right. It was one more shining example of his famous Cleveland luck.

Lord of the East Coast of Florida

For 20 years or more, the whims of an aging tycoon controlled the destinies of every pioneer on the Treasure Coast. Pineapple planters in the sparsely settled communities of Stuart, Jensen, Fort Pierce and Vero Beach lived in the sun and shadow of his empire. All the other farmers and fishermen did, too. In fact, everyone along the entire length of the frontier peninsula was beholden to one man for the fruits of advancing civilization. In the final decades of his life, Henry Morrison Flagler was lord of the East Coast of Florida.

In America, cash has a way of becoming king. Although our Founders banned royal titles, regal privileges remained for those well-robed with dollar bills. The striking difference from the Old World is how many princes of profit in our history have risen from nothing. Flagler is a case in point. His father, a Presbyterian minister, struggled to support his family on meager offerings from his parishioners. Young Henry had to help support himself from an early age. He quit school after the eighth grade and left home to find work with relatives in Ohio. Until he was 37, Flagler wrestled with his own series of ups and downs, including business failure and debts.

It was the Rockcfeller connection that set him on his financial throne. His first wife's family helped. In 1867, John D. Rockefeller needed to borrow money to expand his new oil refinery in Cleveland. Flagler's in-laws agreed to loan Rockefeller the money on one condition: he had to make Henry M. Flagler his partner. That was a business deal that changed the face of America. The timing for Flagler could not have been better; it was the dawn of the Age of Oil.

Years later, under questioning in a Senate investigation, Rockefeller would insist that Flagler had been the brains behind the Standard Oil Company. He said Flagler was the one who came up with ways to control the railroads and raise transportation costs on all the company's competitors to put them out of business. And Flagler came up with the pipeline idea, too, to bypass railroad owners who refused to buckle under. Standard Oil's chief executives made it to the top of the heap by wrecking anyone standing in their way. "It's business," they explained. Ida Tarbell, the famous muckraker, said that because of Rockefeller and Flagler's company, the ordinary laws of morality no longer applied in America's business culture. How you made it big didn't matter anymore, she lamented. All that counted was success.

When Flagler was 48, his wife got sick, but he was too busy to take her to the French Riviera as her doctor had ordered. Wasn't there someplace closer that might help her lungs? The doctor suggested Jacksonville. Maybe the sea breezes there would help. Jacksonville was a little tourist town back then. The couple stayed for several weeks, but business was pressing. They hurried back north. There just wasn't enough time to stay away from the smog and the cold. Mary languished and died in 1881.

A couple of years later, Flagler married his dead wife's attractive nurse, Alice, a young woman with flaming hair. She was wild and crazy—literally crazy, as would later become apparent. She loved lavish parties and decking herself in fabulous gowns with revealing décolletages, where she dangled long strands of pearls. Alice loved extravagance. And why not? Her husband was one of the richest men in the world. She must have made Henry realize that money is made for spending. Suddenly, Flagler found time to get away from the grind at Standard Oil. He had long since conquered the oil industry anyway, so while lolling with Alice in St. Augustine, Flagler began to imagine turning America's oldest town into a winter retreat for the winners of the Gilded Age.

Flagler brought in a thousand workers and built a palace that impressed the world: the Ponce de Leon Hotel. With all its striking turrets and towers, he might have found the design in a book of fairy tales. Louis Tiffany came down from New York to do the glass. And there were painted ceilings, hand-carved moldings, ornate marbles, oriental carpets, and luxury, luxury, luxury! The grand resort lit up with newly invented electric lights as the first guests arrived just after Flagler's 58th birthday in January of 1888. Alice hosted a stunning ball for the cream of the Northeast's social register. President Cleveland came the next month for a stay.

Some men might have rested there, but Flagler had the spirit of an Alexander. New worlds to conquer were always luring him away from leisure. Once a monopolist, always a monopolist! He bought out his competition in St. Augustine and built another hotel with a casino and a giant indoor swimming pool. And when local government officials had the gall to decline his next development proposal, he decided to show them. He'd pump the rest of his money into someplace where no one would tell him "no."

Meanwhile, a couple of hundred miles down south, Treasure Coast pioneers were sweating it out in palm-thatched shacks and cabins. Handfuls of hardy immigrants were wrestling with the elements and bugs as they won the sandy land from palmettos holding it tight. Day by day through all the slow months of a dozen slow years beyond the reach of civilization, except by boat, they clawed and stretched pineapple plantations across homesteaded acres.

Pineapples had a big advantage over every other crop. Not only could those prickly plants tolerate the region's poor soil and uncertain rains, the net income per acre from a crop of pineapples proved immensely higher than anything raised on northern farms. And the ripening fruit could endure a long, slow trip to market. When that news got out in the 1880s, settlers came from far away with dreams of raising a fortune. It was a hard life, but it brought good money when sailboats hauled their harvests away. Later in the decade, steamboats moved more produce faster.

Flagler needed to forge another earthly paradise, and he wanted to get there in style by train. Looking south down the peninsula, he could see that all the rest of the coast of Florida was waiting for him to put it on the map. He hired an army of 2,000 and started laying track. A hotel he built in Ormond Beach barely held his interest overnight. He had to press on further. In exchange for laying track, the Florida Legislature gave him title to vast amounts of public land. Legislators were willing to do whatever it took to bring progress to their long-forgotten state.

South of the Sebastian River and west of the Indian River there was a place where local investors planned to build a town. They were going to call it Wauregan. If Flagler built one of his fabulous hotels there, they thought that was just what they needed to get things off the ground. When Flagler saw their plans, he said he might build a hotel there, but on one condition: they'd have to give him ownership of every lot in town. Nothing was ever done.

Flagler was too rich and powerful to waste time on compromise. He was busy building a world where he would always get his way. When his son Harry dared to express his own will—Harry wanted to pursue music instead of business—Flagler kicked him out and never spoke to him again. And when Alice went completely over the edge, consulting astral spirits with her Ouija board—the spirits told her she belonged with the Russian Czar—he committed her to an insane asylum for the last 33 years of her life. To please the state's most powerful new citizen, Florida's legislature changed the statutes prohibiting divorce to allow Flagler to escape the bonds of marriage.

Flagler wanted his next building site to match his vision of tropical paradise. He bypassed the scrubby pineapple fields of the Treasure Coast in favor of coconut palms. Years before, a shipwreck spilled 20,000 coconuts from Trinidad along the coast where Flagler created

Palm Beach. The trees that grew from those giant seeds attracted the magnate to that locale. He constructed the biggest wooden structure in the world there: the Royal Poinciana Hotel. It had seven miles of hallways running through six stories of elegance. He built The Breakers, too. On the other side of the water, he created the town of West Palm Beach for his "help." The power plant for his hotel needed 25 tons of coal per day to keep the lights on, so, he had to build a railroad to ship in supplies and provide transportation for his guests.

It was Flagler's railroad that started the pineapple boom. Business had been good with steamers, but after the railroad reached the region in 1894, freight trains shipped so much more. Field hands moved in as the growers spread their plantations across the coastal regions of the Treasure Coast as far as the eye could see. It made local planters wealthy enough to put up big houses. By the turn of the century, the Treasure Coast was well on the way to becoming the Pineapple Capital of the World. Except for worries about freezes and pests, local planters must have thought life looked as golden as the fruit they were producing.

But trouble was brewing. Henry Flagler couldn't sit still. Although he built a marble palace in Palm Beach to live in with his young third wife, Mary Lily, he pressed his empire south to Miami and the Keys. And even that wasn't enough. Many thought that when he built his train across the ocean to Key West he had gone completely mad. Flagler's Folly, they called it. Some still think it was one man's romantic quest to conquer nature, just because he could.

There was method to the old man's madness. After the U.S. defeated Spain and Cuba gained its independence, the big money quickly moved in. Flagler became a director in a venture called the Cuba Company. Along with cohorts, including J.P. Morgan, he acquired 200,000 acres of that island and built a railroad on it. One of his business buddies, José Miguel Gómez, became the president of Cuba. And the Cuba Company syndicate gained control of a big cash crop. Pineapples!

Not everyone in America was blind to Flagler's secret plans. In 1908 *Everybody's Magazine* reported: "Cuba is the true objective of the railroad to Key West. When the work is finished, huge ferries will carry solid trains to and from Havana; and a through-rail route from New York to Cuba will be completed... Henry M. Flagler's purpose to stake his fortune on Cuba was the direct result of his visit to the island..."

Even before Flagler's railroad made it to Key West, he began shipping fruit from Cuba to the Lower Keys and up the coast. Recalling his tactics from his Standard Oil days, he raised the transportation costs for his competitors on the Treasure Coast, who had to pay nearly twice as much as the Cuban enterprise paid. Flagler even gave Cuban shipments priority over all other train traffic on his railway. Two Cuban Fruit Express trains made it to Chicago for every train with local fruit, and they got there twice as fast.

"The Fruit Express gave us a terrible wallop from which most of us never recuperated," wrote Curt E. Schroeder, one of the pioneer pineapple planters. "We realized by the end of the season that we had suffered a loss of 5½¢ on each crate we shipped."

Efforts by local growers to get the federal government to level the playing field did not win sufficient results. Although a few determined planters managed to eke out a smaller living for a number of seasons afterwards, Florida's big pineapple boom went bust, not by accident, but by design. Growers like Otto Stypmann, one of Stuart's earliest settlers, subdivided their fields and sold their land to a new wave of settlers who arrived on Flagler's trains.

Flagler wasn't out to turn the planters of the Treasure Coast into paupers, but business was business. Before he spotted Cuba, he actually helped some pioneer growers with loans to get them on their feet after a big freeze. Given his history, you have to wonder whether he banked on foreclosing those helpful loans later on to take their land. Still, even though Flagler's empire brought both blessings and curses to the early pioneers, his untamed ambition set the course of destiny for Florida and its Treasure Coast. Frankly, from a business standpoint, his Cuban scheme did make sense. Train usage by the scant inhabitants along Florida's east coast was insufficient to support the heavy costs of running a railroad. His train system was thirsty for bigger sources of revenue.

Flagler must have thought he'd never die. He once said he had too much work to do to ask God's "will be done," before he turned 100. He insisted on total dominion. He boasted to President McKinley that his domain began in Jacksonville, implying the entire state was his personal fiefdom. Perhaps it was. In 1910, the *Atlanta Journal* said Flagler's name was synonymous with Florida: "If there is any one State owned body and soul by a boss, it is Florida..."

When he was 83, Henry Flagler slipped on the stairs of Whitehall, his marble palace in Palm Beach, severely injuring himself. At the end of his days he was nearly deaf, almost blind, and too crippled to get out of bed. As his life approached its end, it seemed as if the old titan might be ready for someone else to take control. "Doctor," he said, "I do not want to go, but I can say, and say honestly, I am ready to do His will."

Death of the Pineapple King

Charles Tobin McCarty was a remarkable man, the sort of man you would expect to find memorialized with a monument in downtown Fort Pierce. At the height of Florida's Pineapple Boom, the *St. Lucie County Tribune* called him the region's leading citizen. According to the Florida Horticultural Society he owned and operated "the largest pineapple plantation in the world." Maybe if he hadn't been murdered so early in the course of his ascendant star, McCarty would be widely celebrated as a titan of Florida history today.

On the last morning of his life, January 30, 1907, 49-year-old Charles McCarty woke up with progress on his mind. He was chairman of almost everything back then. The newspaper said, "Whenever a plan was proposed whereby his town or his section was to be benefitted, Mr. McCarty instantly became the prime mover in the good work, directing, advising and always pushing."

McCarty had an appointment to meet J. O. Fries, a surveyor. As chairman of the Good Roads Committee, McCarty was deciding on a route to Ten Mile Creek. Downtown was still full of horses and buggies then, but he knew that recently invented cars were coming soon. To get ready for them, he had been pushing newly created St. Lucie County to pave its roads with rocks or shells. Sand roads were too soft in many places and full of weeds.

If he hadn't stopped to get a morning shave at Edward Edge's barber shop near the southwest corner of Palmetto Avenue and Pine Street (Avenue A and Second Street), McCarty might have kept his appointment with the surveyor, picked out a new route to the "back country," and lived out the day, if not a lifetime as long as his father's 90 years.

In those days, St. Lucie County extended from Sebastian River down to the north bank of the St. Lucie River just above Stuart. Fort Pierce, the county seat, was an up-and-coming community, the primary population center in what we now call the Treasure Coast. Joseph R. Parrott had described Fort Pierce as "the only hamlet between Melbourne and West Palm Beach worth mentioning," and Parrott's opinion counted for something. He was Henry Flagler's prime minister and ran his regent's railroad, which dictated much of the business in the state. By that fateful day in 1907, Fort Pierce already enjoyed its own ice factory and an electric power plant serving the local citizenry, luxuries most other communities in the region would not possess for years to come.

In spite of its relative progress, life in downtown Fort Pierce during the first decade of the 20th century was hardly cosmopolitan, as a notice from the local newspaper attests: "Complaint has been made that a light-colored cow roams the streets and commits depredations in gardens and pineapple patches. It is hoped the owner will see that it is properly confined." An editorial described Pine Street after a heavy rain as a "dead ringer for famous Venetian streets where gondolas glide." But rustic inconveniences aside, the area had made tremendous advances since 1888, when C. T. McCarty first arrived.

When he was 31, health concerns forced McCarty to leave his professorship at Tilford Collegiate Academy in Vinton, Iowa, an institution of higher learning founded by his uncle, Thomas Tobin. He held a law degree from the University of Iowa and had practiced law for a year, but he preferred being professor of math and languages at his undergraduate alma mater. It must have been hard to move his wife, Lizzie, and three young sons to the wilds of South Florida, but he was raised to be a pioneer. His father, Dennis McCarty, an intrepid Irish immigrant, had moved his family from Green Bay to the deeper wilderness of Wisconsin by ox-team in 1863, when Charles was only six years old. As a boy, he learned with his father and brothers how to turn forests into farmland.

In a haunting foreshadowing of his own personal tragedy, McCarty once wrote a school essay about Dickens' novel *Martin Chuzzlewit*. He focused on the book's murderer, who waited outside an inn while his intended victim ate dinner. "Jonas Chuzzlewit is one of the most brutal, cruel and most odious of characters," young McCarty wrote, "but so born and so bred and admired for that which made him hateful." Remorselessly, the fictional killer murdered a man he had secretly hated for a long time. "This character is one that is very common in real life wherein they have the same influences surrounding them," McCarty added.

He settled south of Fort Pierce in Ankona, near where his father-in-law, Elias Matter, had already moved with his second wife, Mary. Coincidentally, according to an 1885 census, Lizzie's family lived with Brevard County Commissioner C.E. Chaffee and his wife Cora, who would later marry McCarty's killer. The McCartys built a small home of their own in the scrub land along the Indian River. While Lizzie taught school, Charles cleared their property and lined the sandy flats and hillocks with perfect rows of pineapple plants. He planted 11,000 pineapple slips per acre, carefully measured at 22 inches apart. After his early successes, he published a booklet in 1894 telling other newcomers how they could follow his example. He planted limes and oranges, too. Pineapples made him rich, but he was especially fond of his citrus groves.

"My young groves are certainly things of beauty," McCarty said in 1900. "[They] fully demonstrate what can be accomplished in a few short years in citrus tree growing by careful and intelligent culture…[T]here is no section of the state where trees bear heavier crops of fruit, or of better quality."

Time and again, his fruit won first-place prizes at the State Fair in Jacksonville. The size of his horticultural empire quickly grew, and so did his wealth and reputation. He didn't limit his holdings to the Fort Pierce-Ankona region. He also owned property in Viking (now known as Indrio) where he had a packing house and a cottage. McCarty used his scientific know-how to produce the highest yields possible from the sandy Florida soil. His expertise became so widely respected that the British government consulted him regarding its "semi-tropical industries" in the Bahamas. He published an almanac for the crown in Nassau.

In September 1901, he could afford three weeks of vacationing with Lizzie at the Pan American Exposition in Buffalo, New York—a World's Fair that amazed the nation with displays of what the future held in store, including Thomas Edison's X-ray machine. From the balcony of his fine hotel near the entrance, you could see stunning electric lights outlining an array of exotic buildings, the most magnificent display the world had seen. The exposition looked like Disney World at night. But the magic was overshadowed by a dark event. McCarty was at the exposition the day President McKinley was assassinated there, at the Temple of Music, by a madman in the crowd.

In 1902, McCarty built a beautiful home on the river in Eldred, a riverside community north of Ankona and south of Fort Pierce. The *Florida Star* of Titusville described the house as "one of the most imposing residences in the pineapple region...furnished in the most lavish manner." He and Lizzie christened their new home with what the newspaper said was "one of the most brilliant social affairs occurring on the east coast for some time." The first floor was built with arches and sliding doors designed to open into one large room for entertaining and all was decorated with palms, evergreens and "the most exquisite roses." Two hundred guests were served a sumptuous dinner, 40 at a time. Some came from as far away as Jacksonville. Japanese lanterns lit the grounds and "moonlight produced an enchanting effect."

Down the sandy road in Ankona lived a fellow fruit grower, who would shoot McCarty five years later. William Charles Rawlinson, also known as Willie or W.C., was younger and less ambitious than his rich, distinguished neighbor, but he had pride, the kind that spurs resentment. He was distantly related to an antebellum governor of South Carolina, but insanity ran through that bloodline, as his lawyers would later try to prove. Willie Rawlinson made it known via the newspaper's society page that his brother, Jody, held a position of prominence in South Carolina's government. The boast didn't elevate his local standing much. As a newspaper later reported, it was widely known that Rawlinson's 100 acres were not acquired "through his own industry." He gained his real estate holdings by marrying Cora Chaffee, the county commissioner's widow, who was much older than Willie. And he didn't work his land very hard; he only maintained 30 acres of plantings. Until the shooting, the future murderer's peers considered him to be "a harmless man," although it was whispered that he had a drinking problem.

McCarty filled the last years of his life with more land acquisitions, successful enterprises and lots of community service. Those were the biggest years of the region's pineapple production, but a fruit empire wasn't enough to keep the Pineapple King busy. He served as president of the local Board of Trade; bank director and largest shareholder in the Bank of Fort Pierce and a partner in Dittmar & McCarty, a real estate and insurance company. He was also president of the state's prestigious Florida Horticultural Society, which met in Jacksonville. He organized their conventions and lectured secretaries of agriculture from across the nation. On top of all of that, McCarty had a busy law practice. In a land of melting-hot sun and merciless mosquitoes, in an era of long-sleeved finery, no air conditioning, and constant perspiration, where did the man find his relentless energy? It seems he never slowed.

Four months prior to his own shooting, McCarty used his oratorical skills to argue self-defense in a murder trial with facts eerily similar to those surrounding his own death. Neptune Newsome, a local furniture dealer's son, shot another boy out on a busy street downtown. The dead boy had no gun. At the outset of the trial the local newspaper reported: "C.T. McCarty, of Fort Pierce, fired the opening gun for the defense and all St. Lucie County readers know his ability to command language."

McCarty and his co-counsel, Otis R. Parker, were successful that day. The defendant went free and moved away to Fort Meade in Polk County with his parents. McCarty and Parker also teamed up to win another case when they defended a county commissioner, who allegedly attempted to murder another local attorney.

Meanwhile, Rawlinson made a few appearances in the social news during the last years of McCarty's life. He ordered a nice carriage for his wife from a manufacturer in South Carolina, and he attended her Eastern Star meetings as the club's doorkeeper. One time he took his wife to see the paradise Henry Flagler had built in Palm Beach. Oh, and on August 11, 1905, the newspaper reported an unusual accident. It sounded like a slapstick gag. Rawlinson was coming back from St. Augustine on the train, walking to the parlor car, when—whoops—he slipped on a banana peel. With the full weight of his flying body, he landed on his head. Who can say if that bump on the noggin might have loosened a screw, hastening the growing "nuttiness" his wife Cora later testified she observed? Those were the days before CAT scans, MRIs, and personal injury lawsuits. No one examined the internal damage or his secret psychological unrest.

On January 11, 1907, three weeks before the murder, the *St. Lucie County Tribune* reported in front-page headlines that fortune had smiled upon W. C. Rawlinson. A member of French royalty had signed a contract to buy his "fine property" for a bunch of money. It must have looked to Willie like his big dreams had come true. According to the *East Coast Advocate*, he quickly headed up to Titusville to look over some new land where he planned to relocate and grow a peach orchard. In a bizarre coincidence, that same newspaper reported the finishing touches had been put on the new St. Lucie County jail, except for an iron stairway that had yet to arrive.

Before the month was out, Rawlinson was destined to be the jail's first prisoner.

A week later, McCarty signed a contract of his own to add 620 more acres to his vast holdings. He was paying a lot less money for that big acreage than Rawlinson was trying to sell his measly 100 acres for. Unfortunately, at the same time, McCarty agreed to be Count Malabri's attorney in the Rawlinson transaction. That was a deal that would end his life.

This is how two very different lives suddenly unraveled. New York native Peter P. Cobb, the proprietor of the famous general store in downtown Fort Pierce, claimed Rawlinson owed him $1,000. (That would be around $25,000 today). He slapped a lien on Rawlinson's property. McCarty, as the buyer's attorney, made a title objection, holding up the sale. McCarty also questioned whether Rawlinson's property might be six acres short of what had been represented in his contract. McCarty demanded to see a survey to prove Rawlinson's land was as big as he said it was. Rawlinson became unhinged.

He told witnesses he that wanted to kill somebody, and he set his sight on P. P. Cobb. Early on the morning of Wednesday, January 30, 1907, he loaded his pistol and went to town. Like clockwork, Cobb ate breakfast every morning at the Atlantic Hotel. The killer waited for him there, outside on the street, but the 49-year-old merchant never showed up. On that particular morning Cobb's parents needed his help getting them to the railroad station on time.

Eventually, the hard-luck assassin spotted McCarty walking down the street. Rawlinson decided to make his buyer's attorney the substitute sacrifice to his rage. He wanted a public execution, and the attorney who helped ruin his land deal would do. If Cobb had showed up for breakfast at his usual time, he probably would have been shot already, but the hand of fate reached out for McCarty instead. The killer followed his second choice into Edge's Barber Shop. In and out of the cozy shop the murderer strolled, sizing up his prey. Then he waited outside at the entrance to the drugstore next door.

Those would be the final moments of normalcy in Charles McCarty's life: enjoying an old-fashioned shave. Edward Edge's shop had been open for a couple of years. The young barber from North Carolina loved talking politics. He had just won a seat on the Town Council with McCarty's oldest son, Dan, and presumably the topic was bandied about.

Imagine the young barber giving a straight razor a series of thwacks back and forth against a thick leather strap until the edge was sharp enough to melt whiskers. McCarty leans back and rests under the protection of a warm cloth moistening his day-old growth of beard. The barber swishes his badger brush in a mug, stirring up a stiff white coat of foam. Lather from the glycerin soap smells earthy, herbal, not too sweet—maybe a hint of lime.

What could be more dangerous than a straight razor's edge? The slightest motion sideways will draw blood. But you have such perfect trust in your barber's skill, such faith in his steady hand. You never flinch, you just enjoy, even as the blade is at your throat, scraping the velvet coat of cream that smells so delightful, so reassuring. And all the while, the chatty barber divulges a litany of the latest gossip. A brace of aftershave is patted on your cheeks. The ritual is done.

As McCarty rose from the swivel chair, each farewell second of chitchat drew out the final sweetness from the rind of his short life. Outside the door, his luck-of-the-draw executioner impatiently fingered a steel trigger in his pocket.

Walking outside into the brisk air, he found Florida at its best—it was a January morning—9:15 A.M. McCarty turned to go up the street, but he didn't get far. Rawlinson wasted no time. He fired immediately from five feet away. The first bullet struck the victim's back and knocked him to the ground. The metal lodged in the flesh under his right shoulder blade. McCarty took a second bullet in the back of the head not far from his right ear. That's when he flipped over and faced his killer, who stood above him emptying the rest of the chambers of his pistol, but Rawlinson missed every time, except for a shot through the calf of McCarty's left leg. Seven witnesses saw it all.

As the townsfolk all came running to McCarty's aid, the killer simply walked away. He was twirling his gun like a dime-novel outlaw—Billy the Kid or Jesse James. No one dared get in his way. Down the street and around the corner he sauntered. When he reached the meat market, he summoned the new sheriff, Dan Carlton, to come and arrest him. Sheriff Carlton himself would be gunned down on a nearby sidewalk less than a decade later.

Two young doctors tended to McCarty, while he repeatedly called for Lizzie, who was in town visiting Mrs. A. K. Wilson, the publisher's wife. McCarty kept asking why Rawlinson would shoot him. He wanted to make sure the criminal was captured.

When his wife arrived at his side, a decision was made to move him to Dan's big house on the other side of town, the house Charles gave his eldest son as a wedding present in 1905. It was the house where his grandson, a future governor of Florida, Dan McCarty, Jr., would be born and raised.

A telegram was sent to J. R. Parrott asking if one of Flagler's doctors in St. Augustine could hurry down on a special train with the hospital's new X-ray machine. Parrott sent a surgeon up from Palm Beach by a "fast boat" instead, but he didn't arrive in time. McCarty died at 1:45 P.M.

Rawlinson's connections in South Carolina turned out to be big-time, after all. Senator Francis Hopkins Weston, a 40-year-old cotton-planting lawyer and a leader of the Confederate Sons of Veterans, whose elocutionary skills were admired throughout the South, came down to defend the accused. Weston himself had shot his cousin in the head at point-blank range outside the opera house in Columbia; the bullet ricocheted off the man's skull. He knew something about insanity, too, because he chaired the legislative committee overseeing South Carolina's state mental hospital. Curiously, McCarty's colleague, Otis R. Parker, was also part of Rawlinson's defense team. Employing a *whatever-works* plan of action, the defense attorneys inconsistently argued both insanity and self-defense.

According to the newspapers, there could not have been a clearer case of guilt. Three witnesses said they heard Rawlinson say he was going to shoot somebody, and seven more testified that they saw him do it. When he was arrested, he boasted to Sheriff Carlton that he regretted not killing P. P. Cobb and Count Malabri's purchase agent as well.

The prosecution brought down the nation's leading expert on insanity from Johns Hopkins in Baltimore, and he testified Rawlinson was perfectly sane. In the eyes of the press it was time to build the gallows, but the press never gets to tie the noose. Justice places her faith in the hands of 12 random electors. She always rolls the dice with them.

On the witness stand, Rawlinson claimed that he just knew that McCarty planned to rob him of his land and take his life. He said the dead man had persecuted him for 14 years. He claimed McCarty had driven him crazy, but he didn't explain how. On the morning in question, he said he thought the lawyer pulled a gun on him, so he shot him in self-defense. And after that first shot, he said, he blacked out completely, gaining consciousness three hours later, when Cora visited him in jail.

There was no corroborating evidence for the defense. McCarty only had a penknife in his pocket when he was gunned down from behind. No evidence was offered to indicate McCarty had ever done Rawlinson wrong, except to sue him twice on behalf of creditors.

No hard evidence was entered to prove the defendant was legally insane, that he didn't know right from wrong when he pulled the trigger. The defense only offered idle speculation from a family doctor: two distant relatives had lost their minds, and his sister had died of melancholia. Somehow those few straws of conjecture were enough for six of the 12 jurors to grasp and hold onto. They voted for acquittal and stuck to their guns.

With the jury's vote deadlocked at six to six for murder in the first degree, a mistrial should have been declared. The case should have been tried again. But on its own initiative, the jury came up with a compromise verdict of manslaughter. The jurors had no legal right to reduce the charges, but they did it anyway; and Judge Minor S. Jones went along with the deal. The *Jacksonville Metropolis* reported that the community thought the verdict was "an outrage."

Judge Jones sentenced Rawlinson to 10 years of hard labor, and the defense team appealed, on the grounds that the verdict was supposed to be for a death penalty offense or nothing. After months of waiting around in the new county jail, and confusion about the results of additional sanity hearings, Rawlinson was sent away. But where did he go? One newspaper report said he was sent to do hard labor in Ocala, but the 1910 census-taker found him confined as an inmate at Florida's State Hospital for the criminally insane in Chattahoochee.

By that time Cora was dead and her property in Ankona had been sold. According to the 1920 census, Rawlinson was back at home in Eastover, South Carolina, free and living with his mother and sisters. Ironically, he spent the later years of his life working out a strange sort of penance on a chain gang, but not as a prisoner. He got a job as a prison guard working at Chain Gang Camp Number 1. What thoughts must have revolved in his mind sometimes during the long hours of the long years clanking by to the sound of other men's chains? Rawlinson never remarried. He died 34 years after the murder, when he was nearly 79. To this day, the thoroughfare in Eastover where he worked is still called Chain Gang Road.

It seems unfair for McCarty to have faded from the pages of our history. When he died, the *St. Lucie County Tribune* called his loss to

Fort Pierce, St. Lucie County and all of Florida "irreparable." The newspaper proclaimed, "No other man, perhaps, was so closely identified with the advancement and development of this section and the general progress of the State." When he was murdered, McCarty was nearly five years younger than Henry Flagler was when Flagler began building his hotel and railroad empire. As successful as he had already been, he might have stood at the threshold of an empire of his own.

McCarty was the sort of man who molds the world to fit his own conceptions, the sort of person who sets the tune to which all others dance. Who knows how far his untiring ambition might have taken him, if the dark edge of unreason had not cut him down?

History is engraved in facts—unchangeable, sometimes terrible facts. But can we ever stop wondering how an altered moment here or there might have changed the world? Can we ever stop asking, "what if?" The story of Charles T. McCarty seems like a passage from Ecclesiastes, where the righteous man is cut down, while the wicked still lives on; and you wonder what this world is all about.

With his wealth, his intellect, his persuasiveness and energy, there was nothing to stop him from reaching ever higher toward another summit of human achievement. Nothing—except mortality. Nothing—except irrationality. Nothing—except a madman with a gun.

The Pelican Precedent

Statue of Paul Kroegel in Sebastian, Florida

In the late 1800s fashion created a market for feathers—lots and lots of feathers. Feathers possessed a magical power only fashion could bestow. They made Victorian women beautiful, or at least they were supposed to look more striking under a waft of dazzling plumage. Naturally, feathers became *must-have* adornments on ladies' hats, and hats were an essential article of everyday clothing back then. It didn't take long for milliners and the hunters who supplied them to figure out that feathers were worth far more than their weight in gold. A whole industry of plumassiers sprang up to fill the craving. Soon lots of freelance marksmen saw profits gliding on breezes and singing in trees. No bird in the land was safe. Any opportunist with a gun and good aim could make good money.

The fad could have spelled extinction for many species, but the magnitude of the nationwide slaughter incited a movement running counter to the feather-crazed culture. The movement consisted of an undercurrent of nature-lovers, who insisted feathers looked better on birds than in *haute couture*. That's why the first Audubon Society came into being in 1886 at the urging of the editor of the magazine *Forest and Stream*. The American Ornithologist's Union was formed too, and for a while it became the better known conservationist organization of that era. Frank M. Chapman, a popular author of bird-watching books, became a leading member. Chapman, who would become a driving force in the effort to save brown pelicans, worked at the American Museum of Natural History in New York City, an institution co-founded by Theodore Roosevelt's father.

Sportsmen, like young Teddy Roosevelt, joined the ranks of conservationists, because they realized trigger-happy marketers might soon wipe out hunting opportunities for everyone. Buffaloes had already vanished from the frontier at an alarming rate; and the senseless slaughter of millions of passenger pigeons made it clear that any species, bountiful or not, could be massacred into extinction. But it wasn't just game birds that Roosevelt wanted to protect. From a young age, the scion of one of the nation's wealthiest families was enthralled by the music and grace of America's feathered jewels. Whenever he could, he spent weeks in the woods studying all kinds of birds in their natural habitat. Although he would one day become the avian world's most powerful defender, at the start of the so-called "Feather Wars," Roosevelt did not yet wield the "big stick" with which he later badgered opponents when he was president.

When the war for public opinion began, most Americans were on the side of plume hunters and the fashion industry. In a land of endless plenty, few could conceptualize how unchecked waste and plunder might eventually exhaust our national resources. It would take time to teach Victorians that their passion for exotic plumage was self-destructive and feather-brained. As consumer demand spiraled, the continued existence of birds in the wild teetered on the balance of human whims.

In the early 1880s, the Treasure Coast was sparsely populated, at least by *homo sapiens*. The natural order of the natural world cycled through its normal stages with little need for Mother Nature to adapt to the constant tinkering of her errant man-child. Quietly, brown pelicans soared on sea breezes as they had for uncounted eons. Then as now, shifting barrier islands penciled the eastern edge onto a wide sound that stretches more than 150 miles down the east coast of Florida. Although it is not technically a river at all, maps have always called it one. Spaniards named it *Rio de Ais*; the English called it the *Indian River*. It was richly filled with birds and fish and game.

Remarkably, the Ais Indians—an especially hostile and primitive tribe—never decimated the animal realm in their domain. They co-existed with other elements of the natural order for hundreds—some say *thousands*—of years; albeit much less comfortably than ourselves. Was it lack of ambition or know-how that made them leave the region as they found it? When they disappeared in the 1700s, the only monuments left to their lost history were *middens*: mounds of oyster shells, burial items, and refuse heaped up here and there. One of the largest Indian mounds in Florida was located where the wide Indian River narrows, several miles south of present-day Sebastian. It stood within plain sight of tiny Pelican Island. Some anthropologists have recently conjectured that the largest city of the Ais must have been located nearby.

No one knows how many generations it took the Ais, or their predecessors, to build their massive bluff of shells, bones, and sand. It grew to a length of 1,000 feet and was more than 400 feet wide. It was at least as high as the tallest palms—40 or 50 feet. Against the flatlands of the mainland it must have looked imposing. A trader named John Barker was thought to have lived on top of that ancient mound in the 1840s, when a small colony of settlers tried to tame the lower Indian River. That's why it was known for years as Barker's Bluff.

In 1849, Barker was murdered by a marauding band of drunken Seminoles, some say in retaliation for selling them watered-down whiskey. The killing was rumored to have been so gruesome that the entire Indian River Armed Occupation Colony disbanded. Practically all the settlers moved back north, leaving the region to the birds. Barker's Bluff loomed as a vacant promontory above bird-filled Pelican Island for decades.

Although there were plenty of other nearby islands—bigger ones, too—-brown pelicans (*Pelicanus occidentalis*) kept crowding onto a postage stamp of land six or more months every year, beginning in November. They shared the place with roseate spoonbills and other water birds. Nothing much disturbed them, except when rare boatloads of explorers passed by and used them for target practice. An ornithologist reported a massacre by river tourists in 1858. In 1879, James A. Henshall, a nationally famous fisherman from Kentucky, also witnessed a slaughter that sickened him as he sailed by. But no amount of carnage and broken eggs would chase the survivors away.

If brown pelicans could write the history of the world, the center of all significance would radiate from that unobtrusive little patch of earth. It looks like nothing special, just an ordinary river isle. It barely noses its guano-covered sands above high tide. According to historical accounts, some decades the island has huddled under mangroves, and some years those shrubby trees have died and washed away. It doesn't seem to matter to the pelicans whether their island stands desolate or overgrown. They will nest in haggard or leafy branches, or on the soiled sand.

For whatever reason instinct may decree, it was long ago determined by forces we don't fully understand that Pelican Island is the brown pelicans' Jerusalem. And year by year they make a pilgrimage to this same rookery, this place where they were born. Overlooked as it is in the minds of many, and to most it remains unknown, it is nevertheless a natural wonder. Some few people have had the eyes to view it so. Paul Kroegel was one of them.

In 1881, Gottlob Kroegel, a widowed immigrant from Chemnitz, Germany, chose Barker's Bluff and its surroundings as the site of his homestead in the New World. From high atop that ancient Indian mound his teenage son Paul could watch the curious pelican metropolis on the little island below. The long-billed water birds reminded him of storks back home. He viewed them through nostalgic mists of recollected infancy, reaching toward the cradle of German fairy tales. In his remote and isolated hours, pelicans seemed like special beings to him, companions worthy of co-existence. Imagine the horror he experienced the first time he witnessed target-shooting tourists blasting away. At the risk of his life, Paul Kroegel sailed over and set himself between the birds and the indiscriminate killers. Over the years, Kroegel's vigil became more constant. Plume hunters were on the loose, feeding the feather frenzy of the Western World, pursuing the riches exotic feathers commanded.

Another early friend of the brown pelicans was Frank M. Chapman. He wrote chapters about them in some of his many bird-watching books. He always had a special affection for Florida's birds, and pelicans stirred his gusto for the natural world. "The charm of every waterway is increased by the quaint dignity of their presence," he wrote. Chapman would stay at "Ma" Latham's Oak Lodge, a regular haunt for many ornithologists from up north. For many years the lodge stood across the Indian River from Micco and the mouth of the Sebastian River. Chapman even spent his honeymoon there, and took his bride downriver to study pelicans in their habitat. She must have loved birds, too.

"Pelican Island is the most interesting bird colony it has been my privilege to visit," Chapman wrote in his book, *Camps and Cruises of an Ornithologist*. In another book, *Bird Studies with a Camera*, he added, "No traveler ever entered the gates of a foreign city with greater expectancy than I felt as I stepped from my boat on the muddy edge of this City of Pelicans."

Like Paul Kroegel, Chapman could see the deeper beauty in those scruffy brown birds, whose heads turn white when they mature and whose males and females look alike. Although awkward and gangly on land, the big birds soar with unmatched grace, dipping an edge of their expansive wings to skim above the water. Chapman was awed by columns of four or five and sometimes 50 flapping their wings in perfect unison, an airborne choreography. He also studied their fishing skills, quite a sight to behold. A pelican will suddenly interrupt his wafting flight at heights of 20 or 30 feet and throw himself to the sea, as if he were his own casting net. Often he shovels a small school of fish into the expandable pouch beneath his foot-long mandible. Tails of menhaden, a forage fish, flap out from the edges of the fisherman's beak. For days on end, Chapman witnessed pelican parents returning from the nearby Atlantic twice a day to feed their young.

At that time, the magnitude of bird kills up and down the coast was disturbing. One hunting party alone was said to have bagged 150,000 birds of every kind. But Chapman discovered another kind of equally dangerous hunter. Self-styled oölogists were raiding Pelican Island to collect every egg they could lay their hands on, allegedly for scientific purposes.

Chapman joined other nationally prominent ornithologists, who were lobbying lawmakers state-by-state and nationwide to stop plume hunters and other bird molesters. In March of 1899 they gained a powerful ally: New York Governor Theodore Roosevelt, whom the nation was learning to know as a trust-buster, do-gooder, cowboy Rough Rider, and larger-than-life oddball. In a nation where politics is treated as entertainment, Roosevelt made good theater. Teddy was full of "bully" and overwrought manly vigor, but the awestruck child was in the man, and truly the man loved birds.

"I do not understand how any man or woman who really loves nature can fail to try to exert all the influence in support of such objects as those of the Audubon Society," Roosevelt wrote to Chapman. "Spring would not be spring without bird songs... I only wish that besides protecting the songsters, the birds of the grove, the orchard, the garden and the meadow, we could also protect the birds of the sea-shore and of the wilderness."

Governor Roosevelt tried to persuade his New York Legislature to ban the sale of feathered hats. He wasn't anti-business, but he did demand reforms designed to curb excesses of greed. His anti-corruption stance made him particularly distasteful to party bosses, who decided the best means of getting the popular politician off their backs in New York was to make him vice president. The office was thought to be a dead-end job. President McKinley, who was running for a second term in 1900 was said to be cool to the idea. Mark Hanna, who was national chairman of the G.O.P. was downright hostile to his party's risky strategy.

"Don't any of you realize there's only one life between this madman and the White House?" Hanna complained to the men who helped send Roosevelt to Washington.

President McKinley's ornithological credentials were weak in comparison to Roosevelt's, but they weren't limited to his ownership of a parrot named Washington Post. He signed the Lacey Act of 1900, which shored up wildlife protection laws being passed in various states at the behest of the bird-lovers. Among other things, the Lacey Act made it a crime for poachers to transport their bounty across state lines, but restrictions were still not strong enough to end the devastation. When McKinley's life was tragically taken by a lone gunman at the Pan American Exposition in Buffalo in 1901, a more imaginative form of protection was coming for Florida's brown pelicans. The new chief executive was not afraid to think and act outside the box. Teddy Roosevelt was the sort of innovator—some might say loose cannon— party bosses could not control.

"Now look," Mark Hanna fumed. "That damned cowboy is president of the United States!"

What was poison to party bosses looked like manna from heaven to Frank Chapman and other leading conservationists. Ornithologists knew they had a solid bird man in the White House they could count on. In spite of the Lacey Act, poaching predators were still in the feather business. Their profits were too high for them to worry about breaking little laws with little punch. Much more needed to be done to save bird rookeries.

According to Frank Chapman's research, Pelican Island was the only rookery for brown pelicans on the east coast of Florida. As a ground-breaker in nature photography, he was able to share his observations in pictures more valuable than words. The remoteness of Pelican Island to centers of national power was no longer a disadvantage. Under the leadership of William Dutcher, an insurance agent in New York City, the ornithological organizations began to focus on protecting the pelicans' nesting ground once and for all. At the suggestion of Ma Latham down in Micco, the bird men hired Paul Kroegel to officially watch over the island, while they figured out what to do.

At first they looked for ways to purchase the island and set it aside as a private preserve, but they discovered it was owned by the federal government. After a survey made by J.O. Fries, a local surveyor, it was learned that if the government were to put the island up for sale, it would have to give preference to homesteaders. If a homesteader took possession, he would probably chase the birds away. That's when the Surveyor General suggested that maybe the president could make the island a wildlife preserve by executive order. There was no precedent for doing such a thing, but Roosevelt didn't bother much about following precedent anyway. He preferred to set it. The idea immediately struck him as grand, and he saw no need to think it over.

"Is there any law that will prevent me from declaring Pelican Island a federal bird reservation?" President Roosevelt asked those who gathered in his office to suggest the proposed executive order. Being told there was none they knew of, he cavalierly stated, "Very well, then I so declare it."

The president signed a brief paragraph confirming his decision, and the matter was done. That was on March 14, 1903. Apparently, it was not reported to the press. There was no contemporaneous mention of it in the *New York Times* or in the local newspapers in Florida. For a newshound like Roosevelt to keep mum about a shining achievement must have meant he entertained doubts about the limits of his power over federal lands. During the next couple of years, he ordered creation of several more reservations, but after Congress backed up his authority in 1906, Roosevelt emphatically created national bird reservations all over the country. Fifty-one of them to be exact, along with a reservation for buffaloes and one for moose. Later presidents followed the bold precedent Roosevelt set with Pelican Island. From that small beginning, the National Wildlife Refuge System has grown to no less than 556 wildlife refuges totaling more than 150 million acres.

In his autobiography Roosevelt outlined many of his accomplishments which he undertook for the economic benefit of the American people, but he noted that some of his essential projects were done without the profit motive in mind, because "… they bore directly on our welfare, because they added to the beauty of living and therefore to the joy of life." Among his greatest successes he noted "…the taking of steps to preserve from destruction beautiful and wonderful wild creatures whose existence was threatened by greed and wantonness." Roosevelt said his executive orders creating reservations such as "the celebrated Pelican Island rookery in Indian River, Florida…placed the United States in the front rank in the world work of bird protection."

Paul Kroegel was appointed as Pelican Island's first warden to enforce the president's decree, but because Roosevelt lacked the authority to establish funding for the position, the Audubon Society paid his salary. His first directive was to erect a big sign on the island, proclaiming it as a wildlife refuge. It is painfully ironic to note that the sign chased all the pelicans away the first year they were officially "protected." They refused to return at all during that nesting season, proving that even helpful human trespasses can sometimes do more harm than good. Frank Chapman quipped that the birds must have been expressing political opposition to receiving a government handout. Fortunately, the birds came back to their treasured island the next year, after Kroegel removed the government's offending sign.

Kroegel served as warden for many years, and it remained a dangerous occupation. Two of his fellow wardens serving other Florida refuges were murdered by plume hunters. Kroegel's service captured the notice of Governor Napoleon Bonaparte Broward, who appointed him as one of St. Lucie County's first commissioners when the new county broke away from Brevard in 1905. He won re-election several times. Kroegel also took charge of local road construction, and in 1909 his father sold all the packed material in Barker's Bluff to the county. It was used to pave nearly 50 miles of road between Micco and Stuart, so that horseless carriages wouldn't get stuck in the sugar sand. A train track was built up to the bluff, and it took four years to flatten the great mound of the Ais. Now their history is hidden deep in the road bed of Dixie Highway. We travel over their bones.

We make everything fit our immediate needs. As masters of the world, we manicure Nature; but so many of us forget its vast complexity, its delicate balance, our vital interdependence. Nature takes a lot of knocks, and so we take its fortitude for granted; but history shows Nature can't take everything we throw at it. Time and again when you factor human experience down as far as it will go, you discover the lowest common denominators are always states of mind, levels of awareness. We share the earth with creatures whose chancy chains of being have extended back for centuries beyond our capacity to reckon. It is an amazing world, this planet that made room for existences as disparate as porpoises, butterflies, pelicans, and buffaloes. Theodore Roosevelt saw that. So did Frank Chapman and Paul Kroegel, and many other heroes of the wild.

In the midst of the mad hatters' reckless fad, the National Wildlife Refuge System was born on a tiny island of the Treasure Coast. Although that scrap of black mangroves and sand played a leading role in American history, it remains obscure today. But that is as it should be. Birds need a place to be left alone. Progress needs places that can't be touched, places that promote "the beauty of living" and "the joy of life" for generations to come. If people remember to master themselves, then whenever November comes the mystery of migration will move hundreds, perhaps even thousands, of pelicans to return. Some will come in the night and settle in the trees. Others will follow to build their nests on the sand, and all will be in accord with ancient rank and ritual for as long as Nature will have it so. And as the years span out beyond horizons of our present reach, the world will always be big enough for people and a wonder-house of birds.

The Timeless Voice of Ernest Lyons

Ernest F. Lyons' books—*My Florida* and *The Last Cracker Barrel*—are regional classics that still remind us of the Eden we've been busy trading away for progress. For decades, the homespun editor of the *Stuart News* shared his awe of Florida's native beauty with readers of his columns. His down-home recollections captured the essence of growing up in Stuart's pioneer days when the rivers were pure and the woods were free to wander. Here on the Treasure Coast, we've always appreciated Ernie as a great outdoorsman and a darned good writer. But did you know that Ernest Fulton Lyons was once reckoned among the top authors in the country? Have you ever heard how close he came to securing a place among the immortals of American literature? It was close enough to feel the tug on the far end of his line. Close enough to reel it into view.

Lyons' big literary break happened during the depths of the Great Depression. He was 31 and unmarried at the time. For five years he had been slugging it out as a reporter in a shadow of a town, where dreams had been half-killed by the bad economy. At the *Stuart Daily News* he covered everything that filled up space: births, dinner parties, sleepy commission meetings, and an occasional minor crime. Lyons was in charge of advertising, too. His wordsmith talents were better than all of that, of course, but nobody really knew how great he was. In 1936, he got a chance to show the world.

Nowadays when no one regularly reads short fiction, it may be hard to imagine how big a deal it was for Lyons to get a short story published in *Esquire* magazine. Although radio shows were capturing large segments of America's pastime hours, short stories were still one of the staples of the culture. Like TV dramas and sitcoms now, people couldn't get enough of them. National magazines with enormous

51

circulations were loaded with fiction. Some of the contributing writers became superstars. One of them, F. Scott Fitzgerald, had a story published in the same November 1936 issue of *Esquire* as Lyons.

Lyons' chances of lasting literary fame multiplied when a book called the *Best Short Stories of 1937*, edited by Edward J. O'Brien, came out a couple of months later, ranking stories from the preceding year. O'Brien's anthologies had been a herald of greatness in short fiction writing since 1915, when the highbrow editor first decided to separate "the honest good from the meretricious mass of writing with which it is mingled." It didn't matter that Lyons' story, *A Congo Prayer*, did not end up getting reprinted alongside Ernest Hemingway's *Snows of Kilimanjaro* or William Faulkner's *Fool about a Horse*, two of the stories O'Brien reprinted that year. Just being listed in the Roll of Honor at the back of the book was tantamount to being an Oscar nominee. A biographical note about Lyons was included. It said the Stuart resident divided his time between writing and newspaper work.

A Congo Prayer is a richly complex and deeply disturbing tale about a near-lynching in a rustic Florida town, as seen through the unresolved memories of its fictitious narrator, who witnessed the scene as a boy. The victim, a dynamic black evangelist suspected of swindling a local congregation, bargains away his magnificent voice to save his life. He ends his days as a mute "scarecrow" lurking the streets, begging for scraps—but somehow his voice lives on. Lyons' fictitious narrator recollects the moment he foresaw the immortality of the evangelist's voice, as the lynch mob prepared to string him up. "I was struck by the fancy that the man was clay and would be dust, but that voice was an immortal thing, imperishable, something which might be loaned to many men, but never belong to one."

Lyons' story was awarded three stars in O'Brien's authoritative book; the highest rating available. It was the same rating Faulkner and Hemingway received. In fact, Lyons' rating was higher than many A-list authors that year, including Eudora Welty, Thomas Wolfe, Marjorie Kinnan Rawlings, John Steinbeck—and F. Scott Fitzgerald.

Although O'Brien said it was one of the year's stories that "may fairly claim a position in American literature," Lyons' story was never reprinted in any long-lasting medium. It quickly slipped away into oblivion. A popular reprinting may not be likely today, because the fictional narrator's racial slurs, so common to that era, might seem too raw for modern readers. But the brilliance of Lyons' story is that its insights rise above narrow limitations of the narrator's racist mind-set to disclose the irrationality inherent in his culture's misuse of law and social power.

During that heady year of 1937, with literary promise looming, Lyons married an English teacher: Ezelle Gober of Fort Pierce. Ezelle was teaching in Walton at the time, and the newlyweds moved upstairs above her schoolroom, until they found a place of their own. They enjoyed long walks along the Indian River and through the scrubland that had reclaimed expansive pineapple plantations. Lyons recollected those scenes in a column in 1956: "You have to walk back only a little way into the sand hills to find an old grubbing hoe head, broken glass turned purple in the sun, bees in the pennyroyal, cactus blooming: quiet and peace."

The young couple found a home in downtown Stuart on Seminole Street, which was within easy walking distance of where the newspaper building used to stand. That's where they raised a son and a daughter. Although Lyons' career in fiction did not sustain the sudden height to which it soared, he climbed the ladder of the newspaper business. In 1945, he became the editor of the *Stuart News*. Although the paper was then just a weekly publication in a quiet, little town, his position afforded him opportunities to express his philosophical ruminations.

"Time is a conception of the mind of man," a 1948 editorial in the *Stuart News* opined. "Man passes, not time. He counts himself, not years." This was not the usual stuff of newspapers in a tiny town. "Be still and appraise yourself inwardly of the God-given moment of being in which is contained all years and all worlds, that spirit of individuality which came through the old and goes into the new, that your flesh within which it burns may realize its wonder and your mind which senses it may fall down before its miracle."

In that same year, 1948, Lyons' novella, *A Blade of Grass*, was published in the January issue of *Good Housekeeping*. The plot revolves around an alluring red dress that gives rise to a love triangle, a mysterious disappearance and a leading citizen's fall from grace. Other commentators have focused on the story's portrayal of the 1928 hurricane, which devastated communities along Lake Okeechobee. But what interests us here is that the fictional narrator of that long tale, Frederick L. Sutton, sounds so much like the author himself. He is a small-town editor at a "one-lunged weekly" who thinks of himself as a philosopher. Uncle Sut the Sawgrass Sage he calls himself. The motto he adopts for his newspaper is *The Voice of the Empire of the Sun*.

Could Lyons have been revealing his own unspoken sentiments—past or present—in lines spoken by his fictional newspaper editor? "[B]eneath those smudges on my only shirt and on my dirty, ink-stained pants—my only pair—was a greatness that others would appreciate someday. I didn't doubt."

The Sawgrass Sage discloses the method behind his meekness when writing for local consumption: "Fancy English? I can use it, but what difference does it make if you get the sense across? The big papers have their rules, but I try to make my stories real. I write them in the language the people understand. Little stories about little people. That's all I've ever had."

In the novella, the Sawgrass Sage still cherished the newsman's life despite how tough and threadbare it had been for him: "I love the smell of ink on paper. I love to see my name in print. It gives me a feeling of importance, fulfills a hunger in my soul... You can be flat busted, with a payroll due, the paper company on your neck…and yet, so long as you can say, 'It's me, the editor,' you're satisfied."

In real life, after 1948, Lyons' career veered away from fiction. Well, sort of. He certainly played the rustic country editor convincingly, and he hammed up his copy more as the years rolled by. But he never did give up being the literary storyteller he set out to be. That's probably why so often in his prose you can sense an extra depth, a special glow of meaning beneath the surface of his words.

Lyons was born and bred to write. His father, Harry Lyons, had been a newsman, too, off and on. Harry was busy trying to get a newspaper off the ground in Laurel, Mississippi when Ernest was born in 1905. Harry, a restless adventurer from Iowa, had married Ernest's mother the year before. Josephine Fulton was the daughter of a former Confederate cavalry officer from Tupelo. It wasn't long before Harry whisked his family away on a trail of evanescent schemes all around the country. Usually, Harry ended up busted. In Seattle, Ernest first exhibited the fierceness of his lifelong sense of independence when he quit first grade on the very first day. His teacher had treated him unjustly. He was so headstrong he refused to return to a classroom for several years, and his parents couldn't counter his resolve.

During the years of his early truancy, Lyons studied the dictionary on his own, becoming the best speller and budding writer among his peers. When he arrived in Stuart around the age of 10, the teacher let him start school as a fourth-grader. After winning a spelling bee, he earned a job digging up school news. Not for a school paper, though. For the pioneer town's only newspaper.

This excerpt is from the April 7, 1916 edition of the *Stuart Times* under the byline of Ernest Lyons: "Clara White has so much time to look around, Miss Geiger is having her do some extra work." And how about this precocious snippet of flair: "Boxing seems to be quite popular, even the girls are learning. Aletha Abel will have to wear a nose protector if she continues to box."

Lyons was later expelled from school in the 10th grade in another locale. That time he left the classroom for good, after admitting to the principal that he thought he knew more than all the teachers. He probably did. Lyons spent much of the Roaring Twenties in California working for newspapers, including the *Sierra Madre News* and the *Pasadena Post*. In 1930, he returned to Stuart to settle down, because, he said, of all the places his father had dragged him, Stuart felt most like home. For a while, he tried his hand at commercial fishing, but life was rough and profits were hard to come by. Eventually, he landed a job with the newspaper, where he worked until his retirement in 1975. He spent much of his free time outdoors.

Real life mirrored Lyons' fiction, when—like the editor in his novella—he imparted wisdom to his flock: "The way everybody is rushing these days," Lyons wrote in a *Stuart News* column in December 1955, "sitting and looking are becoming lost arts, but not with me... I like to watch mullet jump just for the fun of jumping, and sea hawks and pelicans come whistling down... Every mossy spot has tiny plants with tiny flowers, some no more than an eighth an inch across the petals, in shades of yellow, lavender and blue. What are their names? I don't know. I don't think it matters. They're just as important, just as beautiful, as the most flamboyant orchids." He admonished readers to slow down and contemplate the beauty surrounding them. "Sit a while. Be still a while. Look a while."

In April of 1956, he told readers, "Pomp, title, circumstance, position, reputation, glory, the human afflatus in all its degrees and that exaggerated shadow in our minds which we call organization, society, government and other hifalutin' words, alike have no real importance. If anything is important, I should say it is to enjoy life, be enthusiastic, kind and understanding."

Lyons was a different kind of small-town editor. He didn't just weigh in on the passing parade of here-today/gone-tomorrow moments of political theater. Because he was at heart a man of letters, a philosopher, a keen observer of Nature and his fellow man, he spent much of his time weighing in on deeper issues of life that hold significance throughout all time.

In a column from November of 1955 Lyons wrote: "In each and every one of us, so long remembered, are the things we loved, the things that hurt us, the discoveries we made: that unique and dramatic motion picture of memory which exists in one print only, an exclusive production which you alone direct, produce and see."

Lyons used his forum as editor to share his own "unique and dramatic motion picture of memory" with all of us. Sometimes he brought us some unusual perspectives. For instance, he felt a special connection with moonshiners, outlaws, hermits and Indians. They hid out in the same quiet places he loved to frequent. But to Lyons, their "hidey holes" in the woods adorning the river were more than mere refuges from a confining civilization that couldn't stop fencing in every last inch of earth. For him Nature, with her many shrines and sanctuaries, renewed a sense of freedom he craved. "They unlock the mind and its friend, the spirit." He was imbued with the spirit of the American frontier.

Lyons lamented the loss of our natural environment. "Inevitably these magic quiet places will be gone..." Progress, he predicted, would steal them away. And yet, he was honest enough to confront his own mixed feelings about a role he played in changing the world he loved.

"That is the way it is with us newspaper editors," Lyons wrote in the *History of Martin County*, compiled by Janet Hutchinson. "We boost, promote, and push for progress, yet we hope there'll always be wide open spaces and fine fishing left."

Like the fictional narrators of his stories, Lyons was always confronting his own divided feelings, and he displayed a remarkable ability to admit his own mistakes. Sometimes he directed his irrepressible sense of humor at his own imperfections. In 1941, he and others "worked like dogs" to prevent commercial fishermen from scooping all the fish out of local rivers with their giant nets. But he mistakenly promoted a petition that would have accomplished exactly the opposite of what he and his supporters wanted. When he discovered his mistake, he contacted a politician in Tallahassee to whom the petition had been sent.

"I can get a kick out of something funny, even if it happens to myself, and I think this thing is uproariously funny," he wrote in a highly entertaining letter to his state representative. "When I got a good look at what we poor, misguided fools have done, it struck me that we ought to be paraded down the main street in our underwear, with signs on us as horrible examples... It is like the anti-saloon league out campaigning for a barrel of whisky on every corner." Ever the philosopher, Lyons concluded, "This thing has all transpired in misguided innocence and an ignorance so wonderful that it ought to be used as an example for posterity."

ERNIE LYONS

Lyons has left a longer list of finer examples of why he should be cherished by posterity. And not just by readers on the Treasure Coast. When you read his books again, see if you can hear the indelible voice of a writer who deserves to be ranked up high with the likes of Faulkner and Hemingway, not just once upon a time in 1937, but for all time. Or look at his hilarious recollections about Stuart's *Great Fire* in 1916, which Sandra Thurlow reprinted in her wonderful book, *Stuart on the St. Lucie.* Through the magic spell he cast with craft, he turned the Stuart of yesteryear into the "Tom-Sawyer-town" of his age-mellowed memories. Often, his newspaper columns brimmed over with more humorous mischief than Mark Twain could have invented. And often he broached timeless truths with eloquence.

"There are still poets in the world," Lyons wrote in his newspaper in January of 1956. "They are men of gifted imagination with the tongues of prophets. Few listen to them. They don't make much money, so they are not of the elite of our times."

There is still time for a widespread readership to listen more closely to the voice of Ernest Lyons. The *Stuart News* intends to digitally preserve all of its newspapers from the past, so the long trail of print that Lyons left behind will be available at everyone's fingertips—all over the world. The possibilities for him to continue his service as "an emissary to the mind," as he so aptly referenced his small-town editor's role in *A Blade of Grass*, exceed all boundaries he could have imagined in his lifetime.

Ernest and Ezelle Lyons with Evans Crary, Sr. and Talley Crary in 1966

On February 19, 1966, Lyons' local community honored him by naming one of the two bridges from Stuart to the ocean after him. When he spoke at the ceremony, he recalled being a barefoot boy roaming the region before there were any bridges at all. When Lyons first saw Stuart, it was a time before fences. Seminole Indians and settlers could wander just about anywhere they wished. So many images of an altered past must have flashed through his mind as he humbly accepted the honor that progress brought him. He said it paralyzed him to realize a bridge was going to carry his name. "I keep going back to that barefoot kid and thinking: 'Oh no! Not for little Ernie."

The bridge was a grand monument to his memory, but like so many structures in modern America, the Ernest F. Lyons Bridge was not built to last. It has already been replaced with a new bridge he didn't live to see. He died in 1990. Happily, the new bridge was named for him, too. But when it crumbles, Ernest Fulton Lyons will still have a monument that is greater than a concrete bridge. He built it with his words. And through those words his community will be continually enriched. Like the narrator in his long-forgotten, but briefly-celebrated story, Lyons must have sensed the gift he shared was "an immortal thing, imperishable..." Something he was destined to hold but never own: a voice that still lives on.

Crary House

Crary House when it used to stand at 311 Cardinal Way in Stuart, Florida

There would be so many ways to begin telling the story of Crary House. We could begin with the birth of Evans Crary in Tampa in 1905, or the birth of his orphaned father in Cincinnati in 1873. To emphasize the depth of Evans Crary's ancestral roots in the Sunshine State, we might begin with the birth of his mother, Alice Lewis, in a cabin near Lake Monroe north of Orlando in 1883, or the birth of her mother, Caroline Lee, in the more primitive wilderness of Florida in 1856—barely more than a decade after the state received a star on our nation's flag.

Alternatively, our tale could start with the story of the person who lived in Crary House for 66 of her 97 years: Talley McKewn Crary. Then we would begin with her birth in Orangeburg, South Carolina in 1905 at the plantation home of her grandfather, John H. Dukes, a former Confederate cavalry officer born in 1834. He was wounded at the Battle of Monroe's Crossroads and taken prisoner during the last weeks of the Civil War. From his majestic aura she derived the romantic Old South memories she reflected all her life, quite in contrast to the forward-looking pragmatism of the New South politician she married.

Another logical starting point might be to launch into a description of the quaint structure itself: an unusual mix of stucco, lattice trim, two wide gables, and the steepest roof you are likely to see in a land of no snow. When the lattice was painted dark, the house looked like it had Tudor relatives in Britain, but there is Canada in that roof. Yet, the stucco argues the house is at least partly Floridian. What a curious mixture of styles! I've heard enchanted strollers call it a gingerbread house. Well, I suppose it might be the sort of home you'd find in a fairy tale. No doubt, it has great charm, although it looked more magnificent centered in a wide lawn with palms and fruit trees re-enforcing each flank. Look the world over and you will never find its twin. As for the interior—well, I'll tell you about that later.

I think the story might be cobbled together a different way, beginning with the fascinating era when the house was built. It was, at most, an undrawn vision in the mind of its architect when the forces of history converged into that great social upheaval known as the Roaring Twenties. The common effort industrialists made during the recent World War had contributed to a surge in national prosperity trickling down to a growing middle class. Ordinary Americans suddenly felt as if they were wealthy. In a time when imagination was overtaken by a rush of inventions the world had never seen before, most folks had extra dollars to spend.

The human race emerged from the horse-and-buggy era to discover the wonders of mobility in self-propelled, gas-powered contraptions that only the rich had been able to afford in the decade before. Henry Ford had reduced the cost of his mass-produced machines low enough for practically everyone to buy one on credit. Ford's competitors followed suit, and soon all the rut roads in the country were clogging up with noisy automobiles. People had places to go and new sites to see, so the whole nation suddenly went on tour. Now, it wasn't just Henry Flagler and his rich cronies who could escape to Florida for the winter. Everyone in the frigid states could jump in a car and drive down to enjoy the subtropics for a spell.

As the first mighty waves of tourists rolled in, it quickly became apparent to the natives that their visitors had plenty of money to spend on food, entertainment—and land. Florida had lots of land. Throughout the nation's history, the migration of pioneers and prospectors had been westward. Barely any hardy souls considered trudging too far south into the swampy peninsula hanging down the eastern edge of the map. Early cartographers disparaged much of Florida's territory calling it Mosquito County, which would have been enough to scare me away, I'm sure. But the bugs didn't matter anymore, not in the 1920s. Citronella had been invented, and other smelly insect repellents were on the market, too. And a budding advertising industry had discovered the advantages of telling just one side of the story to a gullible public—the positive side.

Besides cars and bug spray, electricity was becoming available everywhere. Now you could plug in an affordable electric fan to blow a breeze through any room. With the artificial wind hitting your perspiration, you could feel cool enough to function. But most of the tourists drove down in winter to escape the ice and snow. Snowbirds didn't have to worry about bugs, and heat, and humidity. They only experienced the perfection of our easy winters. It made them eager to purchase a sunny place of their own. All their envious friends back home wanted to buy a piece of paradise, too. The trouble was—everyone decided to buy property in Florida at the same time. That's what started the boom.

Our latest real estate bubble was a repetition of the theme. We've been reminded what happens when speculation fever takes hold. When the whole world seems to be getting rich buying and selling property, even the sober-minded are apt to jump in and help drive prices up. That's what happened in the first great Florida land boom. If you bought a lot today, you could double your money tomorrow. People bought and sold property sight unseen. Values went up, and up, and up.

The sleepy hamlet of Stuart, Florida was not without its fair share of entrepreneurs anxious to cash in on the craze, but they needed the help of experts. Harry Lyons, the father of an icon of local history, Ernie Lyons, had experience selling property. In 1924, the 54-year-old was selling real estate on the North Shore of Chicago and making plenty of money, but the prices in Illinois weren't jumping like they were in Florida. Florida was the place where you could get richer quicker, and fortunately for Harry, he had Florida connections.

A decade before, Harry Lyons had practically worked himself to death. His doctors advised him to take some serious time off. So for two years of convalescence, he went fishing in Stuart. The tiny village was a fishing paradise nestled on the bend of the vast St. Lucie River at the northernmost reaches of Palm Beach County. After his recovery, he vacationed there time and again. He knew the locals—all the movers and shakers. And now the folks in Stuart were trying to break away and form their own county. The opportunity must have seemed perfect. He could build a new city of his own. Communities were springing up all over the state, but no one with serious business know-how had discovered Stuart, yet.

Harry assembled a development team, including a real estate buddy from Chicago named Don Innes, and another business partner who'd been working in Detroit named Scott Marwood Atkin. Atkin was a 35-year-old real estate salesman. Harry brought his talented team to Stuart and joined in the effort to wrestle away a chunk of Palm Beach County. The developers needed land to subdivide, and they found it. Among the landowners willing to let Harry Lyons help them turn their property into cash were Carroll Dunscombe and his wife Janet, a member of the prominent Krueger family.

The Dunscombes owned a beautiful stretch of land bordering the wide St. Lucie River and a "yacht basin" known as Krueger Creek. Carroll was a planter. He grew pineapples, grapefruit, and mangoes and shipped them north on the railroad. But the pineapple business wasn't as profitable as it once had been. Competition from Cuban planters was fierce. Plowing up his crops and selling his land in lots sounded like a better bet. With Harry Lyons' help, Carroll Dunscombe formed St. Lucie Estates, Inc., and platted his land. A prominent architect from Miami named Gerald R. O'Reilly joined the development team.

The section of St. Lucie Estates where Crary House was located was platted on February 12, 1925, a little less than four months before a brand new governor from Jacksonville signed the law giving the new county his own last name: Martin. Two weeks later a member of the development team, Scott Atkin, was first in line on the ledger book for St. Lucie Estates Subdivision, Section Three. He chose lot number 5 on the landward side of Cardinal Way. That's where Crary House would stand for nearly 85 years. Another member of the team took one of the lots beside him.

By the following year, the developer's brochure of 1926 would feature photos of 16 new homes. All of them showed character; most looked somewhat Mediterranean. Included among them were photos of the Pompeii-villa-style home of Don R. Innes and the Tudor-looking house owned by Scott M. Atkin.

Crary House was built at the high-water mark of the Great Florida Land Boom. The rising tide of property values was about to wash out to sea, drowning speculators and turning the state's economy inside out. But in April of 1926 when Stuart Mayor John Taylor signed his letter included in the impressive brochure for St. Lucie Estates, few could have realized what financial ruin lay ahead.

In retrospect, the perky sales brochure for St. Lucie Estates is a remarkable example of why we now have laws governing the sale of subdivided lands. It begins with a statement likely to make sophisticated buyers of our day cringe: "Florida property can be bought, unseen, with the same confidence that property adjoining your own home can be purchased..." The 16-page ad goes on to tout the "...dry, balmy climate peculiar to the region...". (Humidity doesn't sell). Stuart is described as a "thriving city" and it is said to "...have all the conveniences offered by a modern city." (Many years later, when I was a child in the 1960s, those conveniences were still rather limited. We drove all the way to West Palm Beach to do much of our shopping or to find a selection of first-run movies).

In another burst of puffing, the brochure claims Stuart has "...unparalleled attractions for winter residents." However, a careful reader might note that while the ad claims Stuart will become one of the great winter resorts of Florida, that bright future will only come "...as soon as the necessary hotels, apartments, and homes are built to accommodate winter residents." If there were such a thing as truth in advertising, they might have been required to add, "Cross your fingers folks, there's really not much here yet."

At least the road infrastructure was in place in St. Lucie Estates, and anyone could see those 16 houses shown in the sales brochure were attractively designed by Gerald J. O'Reilly. The ad proclaims him to be an architect of national reputation. In his portfolio, O'Reilly could boast of major commercial buildings constructed in Miami, including a high rise, the Hahn Building, the Shoreland Arcade.

Of the sixteen houses O'Reilly designed for St. Lucie Estates, most were Mediterranean, but one stood out as unique and maybe out of place in subtropical Stuart. Years later, Harry Lyons sent Talley Crary a photo taken of the house when construction was nearing completion. On the back of the photo he penciled a line claiming Talley owned the only house in Florida with a Canadian roof.

True, the roof is steep enough for snow to slide off, if Florida ever had snow. But why had O'Reilly designed a house that Harry thought belonged in Canada? Well, as it turns out, Scott Atkin and his wife Minerva were both from Ontario—from a town called Brussels in the county of Huron—about 60 miles from Detroit. They must have wanted O'Reilly to design a house that reminded them of where they came from.

Evans Crary had never even heard of Stuart when Crary House was being constructed, or when Scott and Minerva moved in to make it their home. Evans was a 20-year-old law student at the University of Florida up in Gainesville at the time. Coincidentally, at the same time Harry Lyons was promoting St. Lucie Estates in Stuart, Evans' father was busy promoting a new subdivision back home in Tampa. The real estate company of Robson & Crary was calling its development Evelyn City.

Perley Frederick Crary had previously worked as a bookkeeper for one of Tampa's major developers. Swann and Holzinger had developed the first big suburb beside Tampa Bay: Suburb Beautiful. In fact, they constructed Bayshore Boulevard, which is still a major road in that city today. Perley must have learned the ropes from them, enough to jump in and form his own real estate company when the boom was heating up. He and his small family had lived comfortably for years on West Frances Avenue, a block from Highland Park and a short trolley ride into downtown. But now at age 51, he was poised to amass a fortune in real estate. Lots were selling well enough for him to vacation in Cuba in 1925.

Perley's father, Charles Crary, had abandoned him and his brother, Harry, when their young mother, Margaret Ann, died of tuberculosis. Charles ran off with another gal. Perley was only three when his melancholy-looking mother passed away. He never heard from his father again, and he never learned that Charles drowned in a ditch in El Paso. So, Perley and Harry were raised by their maternal grandparents, Caleb and Margaret Lingo. Caleb owned the largest planing mill in Cincinnati specializing in decorative wood trim. Perley worked at the family mill until the depression of 1893, when he grew restless and left home to explore Central America.

Perley fell in love with Honduras and with Spanish, a language he taught himself to master. He was especially taken with the island of Bonacca, where he got to know the ruling family of the island: the Kirkconnells. Alexander Kirkconnell, whom he called Uncle Sandy, became the U.S. Consul for Bonacca in later years. Uncle Sandy had business dealings in Tampa that apparently involved the exportation of mahogany from mainland Honduras. Sometime later in the 1890s, Perley moved to Tampa to assist with the importation of mahogany and other products coming from Honduras.

At the turn of the century, Perley stayed at a boardinghouse owned by Grace Lewis, his future wife's older sister. Alice Lewis was waiting tables the morning he met her. After pouring a cup of coffee, she asked if he would like some sugar.

"Just stick your little finger in it," he said. "That will make it sweet enough for me." Perley and Alice married in 1900. She was 17; he was 27. A year later a daughter was born: Laura. And as I mentioned before, Lawrence Evans Crary was born to them in 1905.

Alice Lewis Crary, Evans Crary (Sr.), Laura Crary, Perley Frederick Crary in Tampa.

There is an importance to the Honduran connection, which will become apparent shortly. When he was a boy, Evans was forever hearing his father rave about the wild beauty of that land. So much so that when Evans was just shy of 17, he hopped a steamer bound for Honduras via Cuba and spent a summer there. He traveled the mainland, and he visited the island of Bonacca, too. Just like his father, Evans loved the Honduran countryside and the unvarnished way of life in that relatively primitive region's sparsely inhabited towns. Although he had been raised in what was then Florida's second largest metropolitan area, he was not a city boy at heart.

As graduation from law school was nearing, a man named Edwin Brobston showed up on campus at the University of Florida. Brobston was the city attorney for Stuart. The county seat of freshly formed Martin County was having all kinds of legal troubles trying to raise revenues to keep its fledgling government functioning. Issues of law involving municipal bonds were complicated, and Brobston wanted to find a new associate who could help carry the load. Undoubtedly, in 1927 it was becoming obvious to most everyone that the big boom was going to stay busted for good. In an economy where the job market was dwindling, a law practice whose main client was a governmental entity must have sounded promising to Evans—promising enough for him to make the long trip down to see Stuart for himself.

Evans told his father that Stuart looked like Honduras. He loved it and took the job. Talley, his girlfriend back home in Tampa, was incredulous. The two had been dating off and on ever since they were 14. Talley had always assumed Evans was going to practice law in their beautiful, modern city. Stuart was probably one of the last places on earth she might consider moving. When she demanded an explanation, Evans told her he could be a little fish in a big pond, or a big fish in a little pond, and he said he realized just being a big fish in a little pond was what he wanted to be. So, the 22-year-old lawyer took an office at City Hall in a town nearly 30 times smaller than Tampa. Talley stayed behind in the big city.

If a career in politics was what Evans had in mind at his early age, as I suspect, he must have been astute enough to realize that Tampa was tainted with corruption. It would not have been a good environment for him. It was an open secret that an underworld figure named Charlie Wall ran Tampa at that time. Wall was the kingpin of a gambling game called bolita, quite similar to Lotto, except that playing was a crime. The illegal lottery had been popular and profitable in Ybor City since the 1880s. In the Roaring Twenties, Tampa's rampant wild side was getting bolder: speakeasies, prostitution, and plenty of gambling. Public officials were suspected of turning a blind eye. Even the police were reputed to be on the take. Charlie Wall's hold on the city grew tighter until the Sicilians seized his power in the 1940s. Later, Wall was murdered with a baseball bat. In contrast, a quiet fishing village like Stuart must have seemed like a place in a Norman Rockwell painting.

Meanwhile, Scott and Minerva Atkin were having trouble making ends meet. Property was not selling like hot cakes anymore. First, they had to borrow money from Walter Kitching, Stuart's grand old English gentleman. Kitching had made money in many ways, such as in his merchant trade on water and land, his pineapple plantation, and banking. Apparently, he had enough cash stashed away to make private loans. Kitching took back a mortgage on the Atkins' house as security for the money he let them borrow. Then Scott and Minerva had to borrow more.

In Tampa, Evans' father was watching his real estate empire crumble, too. He was mortgaging everything on the Monopoly board, trying to stay afloat. Instead of hanging on to the cash he'd made on his Evelyn City sales, he had invested his winnings in more land deals assembled by his new company: Hendry and Crary. His assets were not liquid when the bottom dropped out of the market. Back in Martin County, Harry Lyons had made the same mistake. Soon Perley Crary, Harry Lyons, Scott Atkin, and thousands and thousands of investors like them would lose everything they owned.

During the months that Edwin Brobston and Evans Crary practiced law together, Evans reached the conclusion that he didn't want to spend his life without Talley anymore. In February of 1928, some sort of a legal matter took him up to Jacksonville. He drove up by himself and on the return trip he went way out of his way to spend the weekend in Tampa, but his automobile broke down in Dunnellon. Hitching a ride the rest of the way, he called Talley to pick him up downtown, and they went to an all-night drugstore for a date. He asked her if she could take the next day off work and drive him back to Dunnellon to tow his car home. She was fairly certain she could arrange to take part of the day off.

"I've got an idea," he suggested. "We could get married in Brooksville on the way up." "Why, we can't do that!" she said. "Tomorrow is Saturday. The courthouse will be closed. You won't be able to find a Justice of the Peace."

"Well, we'll see about that," he said.

The next afternoon they drove to Brooksville, a sleepy little town ensconced in massive oaks and moss. Much to Talley's surprise, a judge was waiting for them, and he performed the nuptial ceremony on the spot. Afterwards, they tied Evans' car to hers and pulled it 50 miles to Tampa. That night they went home to the houses of their respective parents, as if nothing had happened. The mysteriously impulsive elopement suggests there must have been something of the Capulets' and Montagues' feud going on between the elder Crarys and McKewns. Evans' mother was dead set against the union, but Mrs. W. T. McKewn quickly reconciled herself to her daughter's decision. Talley disclosed news of her marriage to her mother, but Evans kept the secret from Perley and Alice, and he drove back to his law office in Stuart the next day.

Incredibly, the newlyweds waited until May to announce that they were husband and wife. A special party was held at Talley's home two doors down from the Crary's residence on West Frances Avenue.

According to the announcement in the Tampa Tribune, the young husband did not appear to have been present, but he is identified in the story as being the assistant attorney for Stuart. The reporter took care to note that pink gladiolas decorated the McKewn home. And the guests played bridge. Winners received prizes. Oh, and Mrs. P. F. Crary was listed among the guests, so whatever opposition she may have expressed about their union must have been smoothed over by then. Nevertheless, my grandmother's mother-in-law was to be a major thorn in her side for many decades to come.

After the bridge party, Talley packed up and moved to Stuart. She was 23. If her new environment looked like Honduras, then Honduras was the sort of place she never wanted to go. As far as I know, she never did. Sixty-seven years after she moved to Stuart, she told me she still didn't like it! But Evans loved the little town, and Talley loved him; so she stayed. Her 74 years in town were like a transit stop on the way to someplace else. Until the end of her life she wistfully spoke of Orangeburg, South Carolina; the place she spent the summers of her girlhood—the place where she was born. And Tampa always held a special place in her heart too. That's how romantics are. They are forever dreaming of places faraway, unreachable in time.

In May of 1928 when Talley moved to Stuart, Scott and Minerva Atkin were still living in Crary House, although it's safe to assume they probably thought of it as Atkin House. In fact, they owned it until 1933. Evans and Talley resided in Captain Plum's house on St. Lucie Boulevard. Captain Plum was one of Evans' clients who had gone north for the summer. He let his lawyer "house sit" his winter residence for free. That's where Evans and Talley rode out the great 1928 hurricane. Plum's Spanish-style house still stands in the same spot it did then on St. Lucie Boulevard, although now it seems hidden among houses and trees. The wide-open view of the river it once enjoyed is impeded by houses built across the street.

When Plum came back to town, Evans and Talley had to find new quarters. They rented the house next door to Crary House on Cardinal

Way. It was that house with the Pompeiian look about it; the home Don Innes had owned. When I was little, I remember being almost shocked to learn that my grandparents had not always been fixtures in Crary House. In my imagination, I had already recreated my father and uncle's early childhood in the house I knew so well. In my mind's eye I had clearly seen them learning to walk in those same rooms where I, as a baby, had crawled and famously gnawed a deep scratch on the leg of the parlor table. But Uncle Sonny (Evans Jr.) and Buddy (my father) were toddlers in the building next door! Looking out across the yard to that other house, my conception of their past felt upside down.

We can only put the puzzle of the past together with pieces we have at hand. According to a newspaper article from 1936, Evans Crary was elected Stuart's municipal judge in 1929. Talley remembered that first election against another lawyer named Gene Turner as having occurred at a later date, but she hadn't done her math. She always proudly said my grandfather became a judge when he was 24, and that corresponds with the date in the newspaper article. Edwin Brobston had long since moved on. In relatively short order after he had hired his young assistant, Brobston moved to Tampa and left Evans with the law practice to himself.

Back then you could be a judge and a county attorney at the same time. Evans became the county attorney in 1930. The 1935 city directory showed his office address as being in City Hall. Those were the days when the town was so small that you could send a letter to Evans Crary, Stuart, Florida and the mail would get to him. Lots of decaying letters I found in old boxes are simply addressed that way.

While Evans was collecting fees for services to Martin County, poor Mr. and Mrs. Atkin were defaulting on their obligations. Walter Kitching died in August of 1932, leaving the mortgage he held on Crary House to his much younger wife Emma, who was then in her early 60s. Emma Kitching foreclosed the mortgage in 1933, and then she took title to the property pursuant to a special master's deed. So, a prominent member of Stuart's famous Kitching family was the owner of Crary House for several years, but Emma never lived there—or else we might now call it Kitching House. Emma had her own big, beautiful home on the river on Atlanta Avenue near downtown, which still stands unmolested by history today. Instead, for Crary House she found a renter: Webb Ordway, the manager of East Coast Lumber & Supply.

It wasn't until November of 1936 that Evans and Talley bought that enchanting house on Cardinal Way from Emma Kitching, who had become one of Evans' biggest political supporters and most important clients. Believe it or not, it was still unfinished inside. During seven or eight years of ownership, the Atkins had only finished the interior downstairs. Upstairs was entirely bare and open like a vast attic. Evans didn't have the money to fix it up either; not for two or three more years. The family was still stuck with everyone else in the basement of the Great Depression.

Evans & Talley Crary in front of their new home, 1936.

Talley said it was the happiest day of her life when Emma Kitching handed over the deed. After eight years of marriage, she and Evans had a home of their own—the only primary residence they would ever own. In years to come they would own a couple of weekend cabins out on the South Fork River on land given Evans in exchange for legal services, and in the 1960s they would buy a rustic vacation cabin in the Great Smoky Mountains—all of them cozy, little places.

With upstairs useless to them then, the livable area consisted of two bedrooms downstairs connected by a hall with one fairly sizeable bath in between. There was also a living room with a fireplace, a dining room, a kitchen, and a separate breakfast nook, and that was all. None of the rooms were grand; all of them felt comfortable. There were four of them living there: Evans, 31, Talley, 31, Sonny, 6, and Buddy, 4. Oh, and there was a separate garage at the end of their small drive, where soon there would live another resident. Lewis Peaster was a homeless, black baseball player whose fingers had all been broken by a fastball. My grandfather was so taken by his state of destitution and despair that he walled off the back of the garage to make a room where Lewis lived for a couple of years for free. In later years that shelved room would turn into my grandmother's laundry.

The year 1936 proved to be a big one for Evans Crary. He bought the house at the center of our story, and he was elected State Representative for Martin County. A.O. Kanner, who had held the seat since 1926 had moved on to the Florida Senate, leaving the position vacant. Ironically, Evans ran against Carroll Dunscombe, the man who had owned the land subdivided into St. Lucie Estates where Crary House was sitting. In 1931, Dunscombe had become a lawyer, too. Even though Evans was still a relative newcomer in town, local voters must not have held that against him. Perhaps all of his government service gave him the inside track. A newspaper article announcing his candidacy said he "...ably defended the county in the mass of bond litigation which threatened at times to swamp the county government operation."

It should be pointed out that when Evans moved to Stuart in 1927, there were barely 5,000 people in the entire county. By the time the voters sent him to Tallahassee, Martin County only had about 6,000 residents. The hoped-for population explosion Harry Lyons and his development team had dreamed of had failed to materialize. The Great Depression took its toll and left time standing practically still. Evans was probably not entirely displeased that Stuart had not been overrun with new inhabitants. Although people of the time did not use words like *ecosystem*, the natural environment of Martin County was one of the main things on his mind when he arrived for his first session at the State Capitol in 1937.

Alligators were being hunted to extinction in local waters, and Evans believed their absence would upset the natural balance of things. He wrote a bill to make it a crime to steal their eggs or kill them, except in self-defense. He started small by making the law applicable only to Martin County, but in 1939 he expanded the law to apply in other parts of the state. Even though parts of the law were repealed in years to come, his legislation was a forerunner of environmental regulation— well ahead of its time.

In his first legislative session he also got laws passed to help Stuart and Martin County with miscellaneous revenue measures to improve their ability to function. He developed a friendship with a Tallahassee lawyer named Leroy Collins, who was later to become one of Florida's greatest governors. There were other notables he worked and partied with, like Bob Sikes from the Panhandle, who later became better known as "He-Coon" when he was a powerful member of Congress.

In 1937, Evans' parents had been living in Tallahassee for seven years already. When Perley's financial house of cards collapsed, a friend whose brother was State Treasurer William V. Knott, found Perley a government job. For the next 20 years Perley eked out a living as a bureaucrat in the Board of Administration, driving from county to county to audit the records of the outstanding road and bridge bonded indebtedness. For all those years he dreamed of returning to Central

America when he retired, but he suffered a stroke in Guatemala in 1950, when he was finally making his return toward youthful memories. He died two years later with few assets to leave behind.

These lines from an awkward poem Perley wrote in 1941 seem to capture the doleful tenor of the man:

If I had my life to live again, how different it would be
There are so many lovely things that I would love to see,
I'd do lots and lots of things I never yet have done,
I'd have much less of work, and a whole lot more of fun.

During the 10 years Evans served in the House of Representatives and the eight years he served in the Florida Senate, the legislature would only meet every other year. That left plenty of time to be at home practicing law and enjoying life at Crary House. By 1942, Evans was able to pay off the purchase money mortgage Emma Kitching took back when he and Talley bought the house. In time he would purchase the lot next door to expand his small orchard of grapefruit trees.

Evans loved raising hot peppers, too; and bananas, avocados and coconuts. One of Dunscombe's old mango trees also stood in the yard beside Cardinal Way where it dropped its tasty fruit. Evans' good friend Ed Menninger, the "Flowering Tree Man," gave him a Japanese plum tree that he planted outside the back window of a bedroom, which became the TV room when television came along. It bore the most delicious sweetly-sour fruit. Menninger also helped him plant a royal poinciana tree that rose above the house in later years, showering scarlet petals from its blossoms onto the roof and yard below. It died when the house was sold.

I almost forgot to mention Evans' partnership with Soccer Coe. At the time Evans made his acquaintance in 1937, Soccer, a/k/a Charles Francis Coe, was a famous author with Palm Beach and Hollywood connections. He had written many stories for the *Saturday Evening Post*, and his first novel, *Me—Gangster*, had been turned into a movie.

A large, imposing man with an ego big enough to fill Worth Avenue, Soccer considered himself to be an expert in law and criminology, but he lacked the credentials to prove it.

Evans coached Soccer in preparation for the Bar exam, and when Soccer passed it, the two of them formed a partnership. Although my grandfather had been practicing law for ten years and held a seat in the legislature, in his typically modest way he let Soccer's name take the lead on the letterhead, and he agreed to let his junior partner have two-thirds of their law firm's profits. Soccer indulgently agreed to let Evans retain ownership of all the furniture and office equipment Evans had already purchased.

For a couple of years Coe & Crary had offices in Stuart and Palm Beach, but the venture did not go as well as my grandfather had hoped. I found some notes on a legal pad page in Evans' effects indicating Soccer's Palm Beach office was running up considerable expenses. The two broke up in early 1939, and such were the times that stationary was too expensive to just throw out. Evans used the Coe & Crary letterhead for many months after he was back on his own.

Soccer's ex-wife wrote Evans from Arizona as soon as she heard the two lawyers had parted ways. She thought she might interest Evans in helping her sue Soccer for $20,000 in back alimony, a veritable fortune in 1939. She alluded to her ex-husband's "Hitler-like" demeanor and tactics. But my grandfather wrote back to decline.

A contemporaneous Time Magazine article reported that Charles Francis Coe had announced his intention to run for the U.S. Senate in Florida, but nothing came of it. He did, however, establish a successful law firm in Palm Beach. In response to a curt letter from his former law partner, Evans extended a hand of friendship, and the two became cordial again.

During the 1939 legislative session, the Florida Highway Patrol was formed. I've seen it reported and heard it said that Evans sponsored the bill, but I haven't been able to confirm that. There is, however, clear evidence that my grandfather sponsored the Highway Safety Bill that greatly expanded the Highway Patrol when he was a state senator in 1947. The FHP gave him a gold watch in recognition of his sponsorship. My son Christopher proudly wears that watch these days.

Evans also walked a tightrope between the interests of sport and commercial fishermen. Their controversy always caused him the most grief in Tallahassee. The commercial fishermen were forever insisting on the right to use big nets in the inland waters of Martin County. The sport fishermen and business-minded residents complained that the commercial fishermen would scoop everything out of the rivers and leave nothing for tourists and locals to catch. Evans struck a compromise to allow smaller gill nets for the commercial fisherman and restrict the big nets to a mile out in the ocean.

The 1939 legislative session also gave Evans lessons in how to run a race for Speaker of the House. He backed his friend Leroy Collins, who had counted up sufficient pledges, but fell short when the ballots actually came in. Four years later when Evans mounted his own campaign to be Speaker, he made certain that his endorsements were incontrovertible. During the 1943 session, he gathered so many written pledges ahead of time for the 1945 session, no one ran against him. Speaker's races are normally hotly contested. Practically every member of the House salivates for that powerful position. In 1937 and 1939, Evans received bunches of letters from fellow representatives looking for support for that job. Yet, in 1945 no one dared to run against him. That fact alone speaks volumes about his political acumen and influence.

In his first official act as Speaker of the House, in the midst of a man-centered world, Evans Crary appointed the first woman to ever serve as Clerk of the House. It is evidence of the male-oriented exclusivity of the time that the records only report her name as Mrs. Lamar Bledsoe. Following that, Evans appointed a handicapped, illiterate man named O'Neal Levy as special messenger and assistant doorkeeper for the House. O'Neal had served the House for many years without pay, but Evans gave him a paid position. How kind and forward-thinking was the man! Those times were known to be harsh towards women, African Americans, and the handicapped. When I'm reminded what Evans Crary did for people like Mrs. Lamar Bledsoe, Lewis Peaster and O'Neal Levy—swimming against the tide of a social Darwinian era—it makes me truly proud to be his grandson.

In another historic first, on May 17, 1945, Evans selected Representative Mary Lou Baker of Pinellas County to preside over the House, while he stepped down from the rostrum to debate a bill on the floor. Representative Baker was the first woman ever given such an honor in Florida's House or Senate. She was a feisty proponent of equal rights for women, serving alone in an all boys' club, and her views had sparked rancorous debates during the 1943 and 1945 sessions. As Evans temporarily handed over the gavel to Miss Baker, he instructed the House members to address her as "Miss Speaker." Can you begin to imagine what a bold and courageous step he was taking in such a day and age? The Florida Senate did not bestow that honor of handing the gavel to a woman until 1966.

Nowadays, almost no one in Martin County remembers Evans Crary, Sr. At best they know him as a name attached to a bridge over the St. Lucie River. The reason he has been forgotten, I think, is twofold. First, during the 18 years he served our community in Tallahassee, there were fewer than 10,000 people living in Martin County. Evans helped lay the groundwork for the future at a time when few of us were here. I, myself, was born the year when he retired from politics forever. That was 1954. More than 95 percent of our population arrived long after he had called it quits. Most arrived after he passed away. The second reason no one knows about him, I believe, is that he was truly a modest person. My grandmother often said he didn't believe in "tooting his own horn."

Evans Crary used the power he amassed to help the community he loved. His influence was crucial to obtaining funding for the bridges across the St. Lucie and Indian Rivers. His help was needed to preserve the House of Refuge from destruction. His connections helped the state acquire Camp Murphy, a secret Army base, from the Federal government. It was turned into Jonathan Dickinson State Park. His tireless efforts helped Stuart, Martin County, and the State of Florida get through all of the forgotten years of recovery from Florida's economic collapse.

The following statements Evans Crary made in 1954 when he was pressing to get the bridges to Sewall's Point and Hutchinson Island built capture both his character and his politics:

"I am only one of many people who have worked long and hard to get the Martin County bridges project put through. I believe, with the people who favor this project that it will, when completed, be of great help in building up the entire county. I would like to see Martin County have a reasonable and well controlled growth, and a more stable economy so that the merchants, skilled mechanics, tradesmen, laborers and professional people will have a substantial and regular income. I would also like to see the county grow so that the young people who go through schools here will not have to leave and go to other communities to find a livelihood and to raise their families.

"In my opinion anything that benefits a part of Martin County is good for the entire county. We must realize the problems and needs of all sections of the county without enmity or jealousy and must work together instead of against each other, to accomplish these things for the benefit of all. I find that in other communities which are progressing rapidly this spirit prevails."

Remarkably, Evans Crary didn't use his position of power in the state to gain wealth. Even when he was Speaker of the House, his pay was only six dollars a day! Correspondence with his secretary back home, Ruby Brown, reveals the law firm's funds were falling close to zero. A 53-day special session called by Governor Millard Caldwell was wiping him out. His financial situation was so dire that Ed Menninger took out a big front-page news story to start a drive to reimburse the House Leader. At 10 dollars per donor, the goal was to raise $600. The article dated Thursday, July 26, 1945, included the following:

SEND A $10 BILL

If you're among the many who want to show that the "home folks" appreciate the personal sacrifice of Evans Crary in sticking to his guns at Tallahassee although it cost him several hundred dollars out of his own pocket (Legislators get only $6 a day as pay) send or give a $10 bill to Ed Menninger at the Stuart News, Andrew Bennett or Jim Kennedy. Let your sawbuck be one of 60 to show that Martin County doesn't expect its representative to do a pompano job on grits and mullet pay. Acknowledgments will be made in next week's paper.

I'm sure the fundraiser must have mortified Talley, but Evans was modest enough for it not to bother him. He never came close to becoming rich. Crary House itself is testimony to that. Yes, it is a structure full of character, and maybe it is even beautiful in a quaint and engaging way, but it is small. It is no mansion. It was never decorated inside like a palace. It is a simple house that was a home to a fine man who truly cared enough about his town and county to make personal sacrifices. And to his memory, as faded as it is, it is an honor that the town he loved preserved his home from the wrecking ball. For that, I am truly grateful.

Evans died in his home on April 16, 1968. He was only 62 years old. When it was discovered he had cancer, he had but several months to live. While he was dying, I never witnessed him complain. He was as pleasant to be around and just as easy-going as always whenever I came to visit him. It was not long after his diagnosis that he was confined to a hospital bed set up in the TV room at Crary House. That's where he passed away. A day or two before his death, he was still conscious, and though he was gasping for breath, he still smiled when I entered the room. There was a peaceful radiance about him. The night he died, I saw his body only minutes after he had breathed his last. Ever after, at times when I entered that room, in my mind's eye I saw him there.

Two years earlier, on February 19, 1966, Evans enjoyed the supreme public honor of his life. That was the day the Evans Crary, Sr. and Ernest F. Lyons Bridges were dedicated. On that day, his friend Edwin Menninger wrote him the following letter:

Dear Evans,

Today stands out in memory not just as a day when a great bridge was named in your honor, but more importantly as the day on which the people of your community recognized and acknowledged their debt to you for the great service given to them by you through your years of public activity. The sleepless nights you spent, the endless bargaining and maneuvering you did, the hours of thought and labor you spent in achieving the bridges as a contribution to the future needs of Stuart and Martin County, can all be forgotten in the public's acknowledgment of a great debt to the most distinguished of our citizens.

As one of your oldest friends I send congratulations to you, not for your achievements of which I knew already, but for the crown of public esteem that has been bestowed on you. May you live long to enjoy it.

Sincerely,

Edwin A. Menninger, D.Sc.

The time to enjoy his laurels was much too brief. Evans Crary was hard at work in his law office after hours when he first collapsed. He never got a chance to retire. He had too many obligations, helping to support his sister and his mother in their separate homes. Talley often complained that they never got to go anywhere or have anything, because he was always sending money to a family member, or someone else in need. But they had enjoyed a wonderful European vacation with Ralph and Frances Langford Evinrude in 1965. And many times during the years after he left politics they cruised the Great Lakes and the local waters on the Evinrude's yacht, the *Chanticleer*. Life was not all sweat and stress. He had many good times, too. But he didn't get to enjoy his little cabin in North Carolina as much as he would have liked. Nevertheless, he always took life the way it came, and he seemed grateful no matter what.

––––––––––––––––

The obscure history of Crary House before my birth, consists of many more scenes of which I am unaware—except for those few incidents reported to me. One of the episodes of most significance to my existence was the rather frivolous way in which my parents became engaged in Crary House. I was not born with a silver spoon in my mouth, but I think I can say—in a facetiously truthful way—that I came into the world *because* of a silver spoon.

Mary Ann Arnold was the stunningly beautiful 22-year-old daughter of a newspaper editor/publisher in Madisonville, Kentucky. A philosophy major, she ended up at the University of Florida in the autumn of 1951 after transferring from Stephens College in Missouri, to the University of North Carolina in Chapel Hill, to the University of Colorado in Boulder, and then back to Chapel Hill. At a party at UF that November she met Senator Crary's youngest son, Buddy, age 20, whose movie-star looks attracted her. They started dating, and in very short order he took her down to Crary House to meet his parents. Perhaps I should let my late mother tell the story in the following excerpt from an interview I conducted in 1984:

Mom [Mary Ann Arnold Crary]: I met your dad in November. And we got married on February 10ᵗʰ [1952] in Stuart. We knew each other less than three months. But it seems like to me that he started out asking me to marry him right away. And, uh, I think I told him, "I don't want to get married." And he—the way I remember it, he said, "Well, my dad's a judge, and he'll get it annulled if it doesn't work out. So, you don't have to worry about it." So, I thought about it some, and I—but I didn't think I'd do it. And then we came to visit his folks.

Rick: His father was a   [state] senator.

Mom: Yes, his dad was a senator. But I guess he was either also a judge, or maybe he just said that. You know, he had been a judge. I guess some people still called him judge. But that's what he told me anyway. But—we had a big

time. And I think I really—I fell in love with him [Buddy]. And, uh, so we decided we'd get married. And it was the break between semesters at the university [University of Florida], so we had to kind of hurry up and get married, but not in any sense of having to get married. We certainly didn't have to—but to get back to school in time. So—uh, we were a day or two late getting back to school. And...

Rick: That was kind of rash. What did your parents say?

Mom: Yeah. Mother—well, we called Mother in the middle of the night—Mother and Dad [Edgar and Caroline Arnold]—and said, "We're gonna get married."

Rick: He hadn't even met your parents?

Mom: No. Buddy [Wm Frederick Crary, a/k/a Rick (Sr.)] hadn't even met my parents. So, the phone rang at eight in the morning, and—we had called them about three [3:00 A.M.]. So, we hadn't had very much sleep. So, uh, I guess Mimi [Talley McKewn Crary] answered the phone. She called me to the phone, and Mother said—or maybe it was 8:30, anyway, that's about 7:30 Kentucky time—and she said, "I met somebody and they asked what pattern your silver is gonna be. They want to send you a wedding present." And I said, "Oh, my soul!" So, I went into Buddy's room, and I woke him up, and I said, "Buddy, do you still want to get married?" And he said, "Well, I don't know. Do you?" Ha, ha, ha! And I said, "Well, I don't know, but Mother is on the phone and somebody wants to know our pattern of silver." And he said, "Well, do you think we ought to have Chantilly or Strasbourg?" Or maybe I said that. I said, "Well, I believe I like Strasbourg better." So, I went back and I said, "Strasbourg." Ha, ha, ha! So, that was it. I believe if Mother hadn't called, we probably wouldn't have gotten married. I don't know.

The hasty marriage those two young people made with so little planning and reflection did not go well. But that's beside the point. As a result of their youthful insouciance when they made a middle-of-the-night phone call from Crary House, I have gained a lifetime, and now, I have the opportunity to indulge in some personal reflections about my grandparents' home.

I cannot remember the first time I set foot in Crary House. From my infancy until I was three, I must have visited many times, but then we moved away—first to Washington, D.C., and then to Mexico City. My father worked for the U.S. State Department. Then he decided to go to law school, so we moved to Gainesville, Florida. When I was nearly seven years old we moved back to Stuart, where Dad joined the law firm of Crary, Crary & Crary, which had offices upstairs in the Dehon Building. I think the year was 1961. So, my conscious memories of my grandfather, Evans Crary, extend for a period of nearly seven years in the 1960s.

I spent a great deal of time at Crary House. At any given time of day, I would ride over there on my bike from the little house my grandfather acquired for us in a foreclosure sale. Our house was half a mile away on Madison Avenue, and I made the trek between the two houses a million times. My grandparents' house was a place where I always felt welcome. It's hard to describe what I want to say, but somehow it always felt more like home than home—my own, I mean. In my imperfect memory now, it seems like I was always spending the night there. Just like Ricky and Lucy in the *I Love Lucy Show*, my grandparents slept in separate beds divided by a night stand. I had my choice of whom to sleep next to. If I slept next to Evans, the challenge was to fall asleep before he started snoring.

In the morning, Granddaddy and I would sit in the breakfast nook eating the breakfast Grandmom cooked for us. Grits were always on the menu, as I recall. Grapefruit was also a featured item, when it was in season. Granddaddy would lead me out into the yard to let me pick the one I wanted off a tree. At the breakfast table, there was a curious shake in his hands, which I would notice as his coffee cup rattled against the saucer every time he put it down, as if it were making a slow, uncertain landing.

It was always easy being around him. I knew plenty of adults who tended to make me feel as if I were in their way, but Evans never did. He was, perhaps, the most patient man I ever knew. I can't remember ever seeing him get angry or frustrated. His example taught me to try my best to take everything in stride.

Once, when we were driving around on errands, he backed his white 1959 Oldsmobile into a palm tree and busted out a tail light. We both got out to examine it. The metal was crumpled and little bits of red plastic and glass were strewn upon the sandy ground. I was amazed that my grandfather didn't seem upset. At the most, he may have winced. He just said, "Well, I guess I'll have to get that fixed."

When I was a little older, one day I was mowing his lawn with my uncle's John Deere tractor, and I backed over a jacaranda tree Granddaddy had been babying for months. I expected to be chewed out royally, and Grandmom seemed upset when I first confessed the accident to her. But when my grandfather came outside to inspect the destruction, he said, "Don't worry about it. It was just a tree."

I always, always felt welcome at Crary House—even when Evans and Talley were hosting cocktail parties, which was quite often. I could waltz right in and chat with their guests, like Ed Menninger or Uncle Zack—Zack Mosley, the cartoonist, whose comic strip *Smilin' Jack* was nationally syndicated. Some of his episodes included cartoon characters of Evans and Talley! It seemed to me like Uncle Zack and his wife Betty were there nearly every afternoon after five when Evans came home from the law office. They lived around the corner and down the street in a waterfront home on Riverside Drive, and Ed and Patsy Menninger lived a little further down.

I didn't know Evans Crary as a legislator, or a judge, or a lawyer. I only knew him as Granddaddy. He was quiet. He read a lot. He didn't play games with me. But he always let me tag along, whether he was going to the store, or the courthouse, or working in his yard. He didn't ever seem to mind my being around.

One time we drove over to the house of one of his recently deceased clients. He said he needed to take an inventory of what was inside, but he had forgotten and left the key he meant to bring at home. So, he asked me to bust through the screen and crawl through a small window in the bathroom, and then I could open the front door and let him in. Well, I never would have considered breaking and entering, but Granddaddy said it was okay, so I followed his command. When I let him in, he made a special point of making me feel like I had performed a tremendously valuable service to him and the legal system.

I remember Evans as being supremely kind. And Talley, my grandmother, was kind. That's what made Crary House special to me. It was my place of refuge from all the many troubles of my young world.

Granddaddy died too soon for me. I was 13. A child's perspective is not as full as an adult's, but perhaps it is more sincere. A child's awareness is sometimes more heartfelt, and my recollections of my grandfather are locked away in the sense of how he made me feel when I was too young to have understood the full measure of the man. I would like to have had the opportunity to quiz him in later years, as I often quizzed my grandmother about the past.

He is buried on the hill at All Saints Cemetery in Jensen Beach. Sometimes, on the way back to my law office after attending town meetings at Ocean Breeze, I stop to clean off the granite headstone that marks his grave. Evans steered the Town of Ocean Breeze through its incorporation, and he was its first town attorney. I've carried on the tradition and have served as town attorney for that tiny municipality for over a quarter century. It's one of those incidental connections I have to his memory.

After attending Granddaddy's funeral ceremony—it may have been a day or two later—I rode my bike over to check on my grandmother. Aunt Marilyn was in the kitchen, and she told me Talley was busy in the TV room talking to a former governor. It was Leroy Collins. Well, I was bold enough to press on through the kitchen's swinging door and march toward the TV room at the back of the house, anxious to see what a governor looked like. I was an avid reader of children's books on history, and I wanted to see a history-maker firsthand. When I burst into the TV room, there was Leroy Collins sitting on a footstool at my grandmother's feet. He was holding one of his knees, rocking back and forth on the same footstool I had rocked on so many times in years before, when I had pretended it was a horse. The image didn't fit my preconceptions of what a governor would look like at all. But now I know, of course, that governors are not so very different from you and me. Years later I spoke with Governor Collins and his wife at a country club in Tallahassee, and he had nice things to say about his old friend Evans.

Doyle Connor of Bradford County, the former Commissioner of Agriculture, also told me what a great man he thought my grandfather had been. When Doyle was newly elected to the legislature in 1950 at the age of 21, he said my grandfather was the one who took him under his wing and showed him how to get things done in Tallahassee. Doyle told me the tips Evans gave him helped him to later rise to be Speaker of the House himself. If I ever needed a favor, he said I could count on him, but that was a chit I never had the opportunity to call in.

According to my grandmother, Evans had ambitions to run for governor in the 1950s, but Talley told me she talked him out of it. Talley absolutely despised politics. She couldn't stand the mudslinging and the stress. Curiously, on all of Evans' election nights she left town. Sometimes she went to North Carolina with Patsy Menninger to stay at Ed and Patsy's vacation home in Cashiers. But after he won, Talley would be by Evans' side. She was his secretary during every stint in Tallahassee, and she was his constant escort at all the many cocktail parties the legislators held. She may not have liked elections, but she loved the parties, and anyone who remembers Talley knows she was the life of every party she attended. There's never been a more convivial hostess than she. She was the last of the old-time Southern belles.

After he retired from politics, Evans turned down opportunities to be appointed circuit judge by his friends in the governor's mansion. When Talley asked him why, he told her he could never sentence a person to death. That might have ruled out the governorship, too, because he would have had to sign death warrants. Perhaps when he was contemplating a race for the governorship, he was planning to try to abolish the death penalty, as Leroy Collins attempted to do.

My grandmother died in the back bedroom downstairs at Crary House, too, and I have recorded our farewell scene in another small memoir I wrote years ago called *Old Times There Are Not Forgotten*, so I won't repeat it here. She lived for 34 years after Evans passed away. Half the year she would spend in her cabin near Sylva, North

Carolina. Beginning when I was 15 or 16, whenever she was off in the mountains Talley left me a key so I could stay at Crary House by myself when I needed an escape. As I recall, that was fairly often. During my high school and college years, I lived there for weeks at a time. I was living there later on, too, when I studied for the Bar exam. During periods when Talley was in town, she let me have the big walk-in attic room in one of the gables as my own. That's where I found the old boxes of Evans' legislative files and newspaper clippings. I decorated the attic walls with posters, and I had a cot and chair in there, where I would read by the gentle light filtering in through the small window looking out at Cardinal Way. The room was unfinished and boasted an herbal, wooden smell.

The afternoon before my first son was born in 1990, the hospital sent my wife Donna and me away to walk through her contractions. We went straight to Crary House, where Talley and her sister Sophie served me an impromptu meal of country ham and grits, while Donna walked back and forth in the parlor. Donna came so close to delivery by the time we left for the hospital again, Ricky probably would have been born in that house, if he hadn't gotten stuck in the birth canal.

I became a lawyer in 1980 and joined the firm my grandfather founded. For 22 years until my grandmother died, I would take a break from work once or twice a week to visit Talley for half an hour in the middle of the morning or afternoon. During my most stressful times, it was always a relief to step into Crary House and leave the world behind.

The first thing you heard was the bells. Ever since I was a child, we always entered through the kitchen door by the drive, and on the door there were always chimes or bells. If the door was locked, you would have to ring, and Talley would let you in. In olden days, the screen door would slam shut behind you quickly enough to keep mosquitoes out.

Talley never turned company away. On rare occasions, we might sit in the comfy chairs in the parlor beneath a 19th Century oil painting of a waterfall that now hangs in my dining room, but we usually sat in the TV room and chatted awhile. We could talk about most anything, and generally we would cheer each other up.

The TV room was cozy. The ceilings were tall, and the walls were painted with the softest hint of green. If I was feeling exhausted, I would lie down on the settee. If the day was cold, Talley or Aunt Sophie would cover me with one of the many colorful quilts or afghans Sophie had made. Talley was always sitting in her chair, a half-worked crossword puzzle at her side. Sophie sat on the opposite side of the room knitting, stitching, or crocheting.

When I lived in the house by myself, I spent much of my time in the dining room with papers and books spread out on the table beneath the chandelier. The dining room is the central room of the house, full of light in the daytime. It pours in from three French doors. Before I was born, those doors were the entrance to the house; but when I knew it, the doors accessed a front porch closed in by a low-lying wall against which, on its outer side, azaleas pressed.

More French doors attend to the front parlor, or living room. That room was decorated with breakable treasure, like the tiny ceramic figure of Jesus holding a child that Talley's mother was awarded in 1886 for knowing the most Bible verses in her Sunday school. That relic is perched above me on my secretary as I type. Against the window panes of the parlor's French door leading to the porch, shelves of precious glass refracted color that amazed me when I was small. In particular, there was one rose-colored jar with a sterling silver top that I wanted to possess more than anything when I was seven or eight.

"Well, you can have it," Talley said. "Go ahead and take it home."

I was much too afraid I would break it, so I said, "When I'm big, Grandmother. Give it to me when I'm big."

In 1995, Donna and I built a house of our own on a woodsy acre in Palm City. The first time Talley came over to see it, I saw her slowly treading the walkway to my front door, protectively bearing a glass treasure in her hands. It was the rose-colored jar! For many years now, it has caught sunlight in my library here at home.

The kitchen was a cheerful room. It seemed white all over, but I think the wallpaper in those few interstices of wall not covered with cabinets bore printed images of cardinals. At least, that's what I recall. There were glass-colored figurines of bright-colored birds in the windows. The big sink where dishes were washed by hand looked like it came from yesteryear, which—of course—it did.

I loved the small breakfast nook for its memories of Granddaddy. He sat in there a lot. It, too, was filled with light from windows on three sides. In the years after he was gone, the room filled up with boxes, knickknacks, papers, and things for which there was no other place. It got so overstuffed, it became difficult to make room enough to sit at the small glass-topped breakfast table.

I rarely ventured into the back bedroom. It was not part of my regular domain. That was Aunt Sophie's room. She moved in to live with her sister, Talley, in 1972. Sophie was one of the most unshakably cheerful people I have ever known. She lived in Crary House until her death in 1994 at the age of 92. She and Talley occupied the house from late October through April of each year. They spent late spring, summer, and the colorful side of autumn in the mountains. Sophie's room was the room where I spent the night comforting Talley the night that Evans died. And in that cream-colored room, Talley died peacefully in the summer of 2002.

The hall between Sophie's room and the TV room was a place for telephone calls. It was wide enough for a tiny writing desk and Uncle Adam's chair. Uncle Adam made it for himself out of hand-planed wood and rawhide. He was Talley's grandfather's butler. He stayed with Papa Dukes for 54 years after the Emancipation, until he outlived the old Confederate. It's the only piece of furniture I chose to keep from Crary House.

Built into the hall wall is a large cabinet, with several drawers beneath. They were thickly coated with white paint when I knew them. When Evans was alive, that big cabinet was always filled with liquor; but it also had toys and tools, which were left over ever after when he was gone. When I was little, I would go to the cabinet to retrieve a cloth clown doll Aunt Sophie had made. I tossed that doll up and down the stairs a thousand times.

Those carpeted stairs lead from the dining room to the vast room upstairs that stretches from one end of the house to the other. That was my grandparents' bedroom, and it was my bedroom and atelier whenever I stayed at the house by myself. Other than the attic room, a walk-in closet, and a small bath with only a shower, the upstairs was open territory. There was a desk with an old manual typewriter on one side, and the walls were punctuated with dressers of varying heights. Until Grandmother got air conditioning in the late 1960's, there was a powerful fan the size of an airplane propeller in one of the windows.

I can't begin to relate a thousand images welling up in my mind from the depths of my discarded memories. Until Sandy Thurlow gave me this project of remembrance, perhaps I had forgotten just how significant that old house once was for me. I traveled over the world looking for historical landmarks to orient myself in time, and now as it turns out, I am discovering that I used to live in one.

After my grandmother passed away, for several years I still drove down Cardinal Way every now and then. Maybe once every few dozen trips down East Ocean Boulevard I would impulsively make an unplanned turn and ride by. Even though my father and uncle sold the house, somehow the old place still lent me comfort when I passed by. One time the new purchasers invited me over to see the changes they had made, and it seemed so strange to be inside again—to see so many things in my mind's eye that were no longer there. I think the more important part of private history lies deep within the heart.

As I've marched through my 50s, I realize more than ever how quickly time escapes us all. History, as seen from our individual perspectives, is a tool we use to orient our lives to the mysteries of time. There are special places we choose as our landmarks to map out experience in meaningful ways. They serve as ciphers or signs to bring us into contact with people who came before us, people we once knew, and yes—they bring us back to who we were and are. There is balance in continuity. In the forum of history, we seem to share a common consciousness that transcends the limitations of immediate experience. There is more to our days than struggle and material desire. Through history and landmarks that take us to the past, we can join together in common accord. A sense of history, when rightly viewed, enhances our humanity and sets our temperament in harmony with the fate of all mankind.

On Wednesday, April 28, 2010, the Stuart City Commission voted 3-2 to finalize the move of Crary House two miles from its lot on Cardinal Way to a new location next to the historic Stuart Feed Store near City Hall. Donna Dorney, the present owner of the land where Crary House had been located since the final days of the first Great Florida Land Boom, wished to build a larger structure in its place. Rather than consigning the little structure to the wrecking ball, she had offered the house to the city for free, but the city had to incur the moving costs. The next night, April 29, 2010, the 20th birthday of my oldest son, Ricky, Brownie Moving began to move the house. It traveled down East Ocean Boulevard, around Confusion Corner, and down Flagler Avenue past other historic structures, such as the Lyric Theatre. By 4:00 A.M. the next morning, Crary House arrived at its new location. The move itself was local history in the making.

The City of Stuart was kind enough to lend me a key, so I could walk through Crary House again. As part of the preparation for my talk to Stuart Heritage, I wanted to explore how I feel about the house now that it has been moved downtown. Seeing pictures in the paper of the building torn asunder and driven down East Ocean Boulevard was, I confess, disorienting. I wonder what Evans and Talley would think if they saw their home standing next to the historic Stuart Feed Store in a place where one of the Kitching's shops should be. They would, I believe, be pleased by the honor, but baffled by the move. Each time I see it now, I'm still surprised. You know how in dreams everything is sometimes out of place? And yet in spite of puzzlement, you accept the displacement as if it were meant to be so.

One of my cousin Larry's favorite stories from when we were children is about the day I fell through the rafters in the garage beside Crary House. I've heard him tell it many times, and it always catches a wave of laughter. He even spoke of the event at our grandmother's funeral.

I suppose I was eight or nine. We were merrily jumping from narrow rafter to rafter over expanses of open space high above the asphalt floor below. We counted as we took turns jumping: *one, two, three, four, five, six, seven, eight*. When we made it to the other side, we would circle back over the floored part of the garage's attic, and then we'd have our fun again. The last time I danced across the rafters, I don't think I made it quite past three when my small foot missed its target and I tumbled wildly to the floor 10 feet below. That was the last I knew until I groggily sensed my grandmother and Larry dragging my body into the back seat of her old, white Oldsmobile. Cousin Mike had been sharing our daredevil stunts, and when he saw me hit the ground, he jumped on his bike screaming, "Ricky's dead! Ricky's dead!" all the way home to his house on Oriole Avenue.

All night long Talley sat beside my bed in the hospital keeping me awake, because of my concussion. She read the 91st Psalm to me over and over. In the morning, after a night of hearing that Psalm a hundred times or more, the man in the next bed said, "Lady, I don't know about him, but I'm healed!"

Well, when the city lent me a key to visit newly relocated Crary House, upstairs I noticed the sliced carpet was slightly sunken in the middle of the room. Could the carpet be covering a gaping hole between the rafters? I pulled it back to discover that it was. Then I laughed to myself as I imagined what might have happened if I had fallen through the rafters once more—for old time's sake, so to speak. I could just hear my cousin Larry, who is a deacon in the Catholic church, repeating my story from his pulpit as a parable of some sort. At any rate, I've kept the incident in mind as a possible ending for a novel.

I found when I stepped inside Crary House last month it was as if I were visiting a long lost friend or relative. The old house is battered and bruised, and looks to have fallen on hard times. Every room is scathed, and the wild color schemes and wallpaper changes do not mesh with my memories. I'm afraid the place would need some serious love and care to bring it back in shape. Still, behind the black and chocolate-colored changes its most recent occupants made, I can still see the home I knew.

Whether Crary House can ever imitate the home it was when Evans and Talley resided there, and whether it even needs to, I don't know. I sort of doubt it. Time moves on, and history includes changes that happen to us all. Nothing ever stays the same, no matter how much we try to hold things in place with our traditions, our incantations, or our preservation projects. That doesn't mean we shouldn't try. Holding on comes naturally to each of us. At least for now, Crary House survives, and some small portion of my memories with it. Who knows—in time and in its altered state, the house may yet prove as meaningful to others, who never knew it as a home, but whose appreciation for its quaintness, its modest beauty, and the nobleness of its age may yet be expressed in a wonderfully timeless and reassuring way.

Postscript

Not long after I wrote the foregoing essay in the fall of 2010, the City of Stuart began leasing the building out as a congressional office. Tom Rooney was the first tenant to occupy it, and then Patrick E. Murphy, the youngest representative in the 113th Congress, took possession. I was honored when Congressman Murphy asked Donna and me to hold the Bible at his swearing-in ceremony before Judge Steven J. Levin on the deck outside the kitchen door at Crary House on February 2, 2013.

I have had other opportunities to return. Stuart Heritage recruited me to give tours one Saturday in 2011. Literally hundreds of people came through the front door to look around. I stood in the parlor with a display of some of my grandparents' paraphernalia, including wedding china, legislative documents, photographs, and Great-Aunt Sophie's music box. I gave the same quick spiel at least 500 times until I began to feel like one of those re-enactors you find at places like Williamsburg or Monticello.

"I don't get it," said my life-long friend Denny Hudson when I told him about the tour a few days afterwards over coffee. He couldn't believe so many people would be interested in the home or its modest share of history. He used to play there when we were children.

"Well, Miami has Vizcaya, Palm Beach has Whitehall," I explained. "And Stuart has…"

"Crary House!"

We both laughed heartily.

Most times when my wife and I go downtown for an evening stroll, we make a point of parking in front of the old home. It still amazes us to find it there, when it should be across town on Cardinal Way; but we are becoming accustomed to the change.

These days Martin County is filled with far more impressive structures, some of which rival the palace Flagler built for himself in Palm Beach. But our little gingerbread house is grand because of a humbler history she shares with her community. She was one of the few homes born with the county when its people's dreams reached higher than fairy tales. She stood the test of destitute years and legendary hurricanes. And when she became the home of a new, young representative who rose to prominence in Florida's forgotten years, she entertained politicians from around the state. Always, she has whispered of times when Florida was quaint. In this age when bulldozers carelessly reign, against long odds she has survived—and now she is serving congressmen.

How many more hurricanes will the old home endure? How many more winds of change? Only the years can say. But for now, the old house is a steady, unimposing symbol of the worth of timelessness— like my grandmother who once graced its cozy rooms. In this land of relentless forward motion, where so much history succumbs to vandals of progress, it is good when something meaningful remains.

Relocated Crary House in downtown Stuart, Florida.

The Lost Magic of Picture City

Lewis J. Selznick

Some business deals are as big as the movies, and all it takes to make them look real is suspension of disbelief. In the 1920s when the nation went crazy with Florida land-boom fever, any castle in the air looked like a good investment. Even a master of make-believe like Lewis J. Selznick, one of cinema's best-known producers of that day, got caught up in his own illusions. If Selznick and his backers had lucked out with their long-shot gamble, Martin County would have become the movie-making center of the globe. On July 1, 1925, the day he arrived in Jacksonville to tour the state with his sons, Myron and David, no one doubted his grandiose goal was achievable.

"We will locate the biggest studio in the world in Florida," Selznick proclaimed to the *Jacksonville Journal*. "You can count on that; that's definite."

Studio was too small a word to describe the vision flickering on the big screen of the famous producer's imagination. The *Miami News* captured the magnitude of his intentions better when it reported that Selznick was "investigating the possibilities of founding the largest cinema *city* in the world." He wanted to find a place to fabricate an instant metropolis, like a made-to-order set for one of his silent films. Selznick proclaimed his studio would be "large enough for the motion picture making activities of hundreds of independent producers."

Selznick's plans made all of Florida excited. The Russian-born immigrant was, after all, a famous pioneer of film production, whose advertising slogan was one of the best-known catchphrases in America: *Selznick Pictures Make Happy Hours*. His flamboyant rise to celebrity had rewarded him with a 17-room apartment on Park Avenue, fawning servants, Ming vases, and a ritzy Rolls Royce. Like his movies, the short and stocky mogul's projected image was bigger than life. Once, he even had the chutzpah to telegraph Tsar Nicholas II to offer him an acting job, after he'd been deposed. Which community would be lucky enough to attract a man like him?

Selznick's proposal to move Hollywood to Florida didn't sound as farfetched then as it might sound now. It was two years before the talkies hit the theaters, so the Golden Age of Hollywood had not begun. Perhaps it was not too late for the movie planet to change its locus of gravity. But so often in life the difference between wild success and great disaster turns out to be a matter of timing. Forces trumping imagination were still in play. At the moment when Selznick stood on the verge of making his biggest production, reality was getting ready to reject his script.

Selznick was confident his strategy would outfox his competition. Florida was three times closer to New York than California, and New York was still cinema's distribution center. Besides, bringing the movie industry back to the Sunshine State would be like coming home. Less than a decade before, Jacksonville had housed at least thirty movie companies. Back then, the city had been known as the Winter Movie Capital of the World. Oliver Hardy, of Laurel & Hardy fame, got his big break there. But in 1917, an upstart politician fired up his campaign with a promise to "tame the motion picture industry." A growing moral majority in the city objected to disruptive car chases through their streets, not to mention bordello scenes filmed on Sundays! When John W. Martin won a landslide victory to become mayor of Jacksonville, the movie people got the picture. They pulled up stakes and headed for California.

In 1925, that selfsame mayor became governor of Florida, but now he wanted to bring the movie industry back. With 40 million tickets sold nationwide per week, the financial benefits of embracing movie-making were obvious. Like many politicians, Martin preferred the smooth roads of expedience to bumpy backward trails of principle. And now Martin counted a superstar of silent films among his closest cronies: Thomas Meighan. The governor and the movie star were business partners in a brand new venture controlling the South's largest hotel chain.

It was the business-minded owners of the *Jacksonville Journal* and the *Tampa Tribune* who lured Selznick down from his studios in New York, but all of Florida was anxious to audition for his attention. Many communities were flooded with new residents, and they needed the jobs his entertainment business could bring. Chambers of commerce like the one in Daytona Beach went out of their way to woo Selznick.

"We shall locate the studio wherever the best facilities are available," Selznick insisted, "and where we receive the greatest cooperation."

It didn't take long to discover that the greatest cooperation would come from a syndicate of wealthy northern finance men led by developer Charles Apfel, who promised Selznick half a million dollars. The syndicate had control of a platted project called Olympia, located in what we know today as Hobe Sound and Jupiter Island. Even in the midst of the wildest land boom in American history, the subdivision had been struggling to connect with buyers. The opportunity to join forces with a headline-grabber like Selznick must have seemed like the perfect publicity stunt to make land sales hit the stratosphere. All they had to do was dress up the old project with a new, exciting name: Picture City.

News of the glitzy joint venture was huge, and upbeat. Back then, Florida newspapers couldn't stand the slightest hint of negativity. It was practically a journalistic sin to print anything that might slow the onrush of Progress. So, if you needed to know the truth behind the happy propaganda, you had to wait for reality to run you over.

One of the crushing unreported facts about the Picture City deal was this: Selznick needed the Olympia project's backers worse than they needed him. In spite of his dazzling persona, Selznick's power in the movie industry was fading fast. The prominence he still retained was all a big show. In real life, the man was losing a movie distribution war to powerhouses like Adolph Zukor of Paramount. In fact, his motion picture company was already bankrupt. His much-publicized expedition to Florida was a desperate attempt to pull a rabbit out of a hat, and for a splendid moment it looked like his trick might be working.

Over-trusting Martin County thought it had hit the big time. On August 25, 1925, the *South Florida Developer,* one of Stuart's two newspapers, reported that interests operating on behalf of the mighty Lewis J. Selznick had purchased a vast conglomerate of land made up of Olympia and a tract called the Gomez Grant. On the property, they would establish a "mammoth" motion picture studio and call it Picture City. The editor proclaimed that Picture City was "backed by the greatest developing organization that was ever brought into play." Soon the best planners in the country would arrive "to lay out a model city based on Washington, D.C." It sounded too good to be true; but the times were manic, and Picture City's prospects stoked elation.

Governor Martin was happy, too. According to the *South Florida Developer* he had personally assured the syndicate that the State of Florida was "100 percent behind the project." The young governor, who only had a fourth grade education, wanted the county he had named for himself to be important. On September 22, an editorial claimed it would be. Why, within 10 years the population would rise to 200,000 and Martin County was certain to become the richest, most significant, most densely-populated county in the state! The *Developer's* editor thoroughly belittled "doubting Thomases" who didn't believe in the county's coming glory, and he even compared negative Nellies to Judas Iscariot. Public pressure to support boom mania was forceful and extreme.

Things began to move quickly on the set of Picture City. The first week after the new enterprise was announced, the syndicate made $1.8 million dollars' worth of property sales. A municipal charter was in the talking stages. The new city was going to be 12 miles long and 5 miles wide. The metropolitan area would be so enormous the developers said they would have to build four train stations to service it. Three weeks into the project, application had already been made to create the Picture City State Bank, whose officers and directors were made up of men involved in the development itself.

By the beginning of October, contractors from New York and Philadelphia were reported to have signed contracts to build a million dollar movie picture studio and a casino on the beach at the end of South Bridge Road. The plan was to rush the casino to completion within the next 60 days. A work force of 100 men started putting up concrete light poles along Dixie Highway. Although no one seems to have spotted Selznick anywhere, an architect from Los Angeles was reported to have spent 10 days onsite working on plans. Unbeknownst to locals, the Selznick family was enjoying first-class amenities down in glamorous Palm Beach. Syndicate leader Charles Apfel paid their weekly expenses.

Full page ads for Picture City told potential investors: "You can buy with your eyes closed and your investment will prove profitable..." The ads announced that work on the movie studio had begun, and the casino was coming soon. Fifty houses were said to be under construction. Obviously, it was intended for speculators to make the assumption that the movie metropolis could be sold out before they knew it, so they had better buy lots quick.

Just as the set for Picture City was getting off the ground, the world turned upside down. In late October 1925, the roads and railroads from Jacksonville downward became totally clogged. After years of unrestrained migration and development, too many people were making too many demands of the transportation system. Building materials could not get through; neither could adequate food. Emergency remedies were required to avoid complete catastrophe, but the medicine poisoned the boom. Only perishables and necessities to preserve human life could be transported. When shipments of lumber, nails, and cement suddenly came to a halt, nothing could get built anywhere. Countless projects up and down the state—including Picture City—had to hit the brakes.

Sometimes bad news becomes too big to cover up. The *South Florida Developer's* headlines from October 27, 1925, seem to have said it all: State Road Chiefs Refuse to Aid Martin County; Rigid Embargo Goes Into Effect: No Relief Seen.

A pause in construction gave speculators everywhere some time to sober up. When they began to realize Florida's land values had soared only on the fuel of collective fantasies, the rocket suddenly sputtered. After weeks of lagging sales, on January 19, 1926, Picture City took out an ad in the *Stuart Daily News* to proclaim, "We have the utmost faith and belief in the future of Florida." Feeble assurances like that failed to reignite euphoria. Close scrutiny of what the advertisement didn't say told readers what was really happening. The swanky casino had not been built. The 50 houses weren't completed. The movie studio hadn't even broken ground.

By the next month, the sales ads got a whole lot smaller, and the only mention of Picture City was hidden in the fine print. Even though press agents, politicians, and newspaper editors kept on painting happy faces on all the storm clouds, Florida's economy was clearly getting blown to pieces. It took two more years and two horrendous hurricanes for Governor Martin to get real and stop selling hooey. Little by little, grand productions like Picture City faded from memory, as if they had all been dreams.

Picture City turned out to be Selznick's last production; he never made another movie. He lost his Rolls, his servants, his *objects d'art*, and his plush Park Avenue digs. His rags to riches story ended back in rags. And yet, even though he stayed broke, Selznick wasn't broken. An easy-come, easy-go philosophy held the former big shot aloft through his remaining years.

"He envisioned a bigger fortune in Florida, where he planned a studio city that would push Hollywood off the map," his daughter-in-law Irene Mayer Selznick affirmed in her autobiography, *A Private View*. In spite of the colossal flop, she said she never heard "Pop" or his sons "squawk" about all the majestic grandeur and luxury they had lost.

Lewis Selznick followed his sons out to California, where their careers in showbiz began to take off. They gave their father stakes for poker games he played with Chico Marx. He had always been a devoted father, and they were devoted sons. Until David got married, his daddy still tucked him into bed almost every night. In 1933, the once-powerful producer passed away suddenly at the age of 62. Hollywood let his memory quickly fade.

Some people say the Selznick brothers spent the rest of their lives trying to vindicate their father's fall from glory. If so, they vindicated him with a vengeance. There's no doubt his sons picked up a double dose of the magic he lost in Picture City. Myron Selznick became the most powerful talent agent in Hollywood, representing many A-list actors including W.C. Fields, Laurence Olivier, Katherine Hepburn, and Vivian Leigh. And David O. Selznick became, perhaps, the greatest producer of all time, attending to every tiny detail in each of his movies, including his most magnificent blockbuster: *Gone with the Wind*.

Vanity

And what of Martin County, where Picture City's unwired cement light poles loom today, as disregarded landmarks of a grand illusion? Like her twin sister, Indian River County, Martin County was fated to be birthed at the very moment all the jackpot winnings of the boom were spent and the last slots came up busted. It would be decades before the county's paltry population figures rose. But contrary to logic and naïve desire, the hard luck had a bright side, too. The region was spared from attendant woes that might have come with the gamblers' answered prayers. You can read a litany of avoided ills in the tarnish on Hollywood's tainted halo. In the end, the region was not fated to become the Tinsel Coast.

Was Picture City ever possible, really? For six or eight euphoric weeks on the waning side of 1925, it must have seemed like a wish come true. But as starlets, movie-goers, and busted producers alike all know, when the credits begin to run and the lights in the theater brighten, a vast chasm stands between the world that *is* and the grandeur we escape to on the screen. And yet, in real life, the show is never over— not while loose ends of history still await the skill of being tied.

Someday some gifted director may discover the magic of that fading vision and make it come alive, but not as the Selznicks once supposed. You see, those masters of illusion who played with people's hearts for profit ended up fooling themselves. They got caught up in the last gasps of the most sensational mass mania America had ever seen; a mania bigger than the movies ever set in motion. And someday the stirring parable of the Picture City drama may be told again, with all its wildest hopes and harrowing falls— in the frames of a fabulous film.

The Picture City water tower looms as a landmark to an illusion in Hobe Sound, FL

Florida's Great Gatsby Governor

"Who is he?" I demanded. "Do you know?"
"He's just a man named Gatsby."
— The Great Gatsby, 1925
F. Scott Fitzgerald

You would think that a man who presided over the wildest boom and biggest bust Florida has ever seen should have registered a significant presence in the annals of our state, but John Wellborn Martin, for whom Martin County was named in 1925, is one of Florida history's missing persons. How could a governor impress his name on the map but leave so few other footprints behind, especially when the drama of his rise and fall occurred at such a stunning moment in time?

On January 6, 1925, as the upward arc of Florida's sensational land boom was about to reach its zenith, John Wellborn Martin took office as the state's 24th governor. The nation was awash in Coolidge prosperity, and Florida was enjoying the biggest binge. Money and people poured into the state at an amazing—if not alarming—rate. It should have seemed too good to be true. Frivolous overbuilding and speculation on parcels of sand and swamp were clearly getting out of control. But Martin, a 40-year-old former traveling salesman, saw the future through the eyes of the big developers who helped him get into office. To him, an overheated economy looked like the dawn of never-ending progress.

It was the Roaring Twenties, when Prohibition caused so many people to question whether having a good time might be more important than following laws. Maybe it was the shock of all the technological advancements that made so many Americans go wild. The movies, the jazz, all the new electric gadgets, and radio! Most of all, it was probably the horseless carriages that stood the social order on its head. Most families could afford one now. The mobility afforded by automobiles was a phenomenon that took the country by surprise. Suddenly, everybody in the snowbound states wanted to jump in a jalopy and flee to Florida, but there weren't enough good roads, yet. Martin won his election promising to pave the way through paradise to accommodate the needs of new residents and tourists.

On the eve of his inauguration, Governor-elect Martin was presented with many gifts, including a fox terrier puppy named "Ben." He said the dog would be his "Laddie Boy." Governor Martin and his wife, Lottie, were childless. Their infant son, John W. Martin, Jr., died in 1910 after only eight days of life. Martin said he thought a new puppy for "Florida's White House" was a good omen for a successful four-year term ahead. If he considered his wife's sudden illness to be a bad omen, he didn't tell the reporter. Mrs. Martin was suffering from the strain of moving to Tallahassee from Jacksonville, so a physician had to be called shortly after their arrival.

It rained during the night, but the skies were cloudless above Tallahassee's recently remodeled Capitol Building when inaugural ceremonies began. The crowd witnessing the event was reported to be one of the largest in history up to that time. Although the winter sun was warm enough to lessen a chill in the air, Mrs. Martin didn't feel up to being outside. She watched her husband take the oath of office from the safety of her automobile, which was parked near the east entrance of the Capitol.

The oath of office was administered by 75-year-old Chief Justice Robert Fenwick Taylor, who was just about to retire after 34 years of defending property and state's rights on Florida's Supreme Court. With a thick moustache as white as a magnolia blossom, Taylor looked like the epitome of Old-South gentility. In contrast, he must have realized the clean-shaven young man he was swearing in was a paradigm of New-South self-promotion. Taylor, when he was only 14, fought to keep the Yankees out of the state at the last Battle of

Gainesville in August of 1864. Now, business-minded Martin was giving his all to promoting the state's latest Northern invasion.

Unlike so many neo-carpetbaggers engaged in the selling of Florida, Governor Martin's heritage was as Rebel-dyed agrarian as any Cracker's in the state. When he was born on June 21, 1884, in a hamlet that has long since disappeared from the map—a place called Plainfield—his family had already resided in Marion County for several generations. Both of his grandfathers had been men of prominence in the Lost Cause. Colonel John Marshall Martin, his father's father, was a politician and a soldier. He had been with Lee at Appomattox, and by the time the elder John Martin passed away in 1921, he was the last surviving member of the Confederate Congress. His death made national news. The new governor's maternal grandfather, James Byeram Owens, signed Florida's Ordinance of Secession, and he was reputed to be one of the men who drew up the Confederate Constitution in Montgomery in 1861.

Loss of the war brought a reversal of fate for the Martin family, which fell on hard times. John W. Martin was raised so poor, he only had four years of formal education: two at a little school in tiny Anthony, Florida, and two at a village called Sparr. In the late 1890s, his father's citrus grove was decimated by one too many freezes, so the family moved away from Marion County to Jacksonville to make ends meet. Young John Martin had to go to work as a clerk for three dollars a week to help support himself.

Jacksonville had been a winter tourist resort for Northerners ever since the early days of Reconstruction. Several years before Martin moved there, Henry Plant and Henry Flagler ran their railroads through it, making Jacksonville the gateway to the rest of the peninsula. It was a major steamboat junction, too. Within a few years of Martin's arrival, the silent movie industry moved in to make the city its winter capital. From his new *coign of vantage* in Florida's up-and-coming metropolis, Martin was an eye-witness to the wonders of rapid progress and prosperity.

Martin was known to have a "hail-fellow, well-met personality." His training as a tobacco salesman prepared him well for being Florida's Salesman-in-Chief. Early on, he learned he had a talent for extemporaneous public speaking. He loved to amuse a crowd with bluster. Sometimes he enjoyed getting them riled up, too. He first came into public notice speaking on behalf of John N. C. Stockton, a progressive candidate in the 1914 U. S. Senate race against incumbent Duncan U. Fletcher. That's when he made a name for himself in local politics. In 1917, Jacksonville Mayor J.E.C. Bowden complained that no one had ever heard of the salesman Martin until he "suddenly jumped into notoriety three years ago in vilifying Duncan U. Fletcher."

The year 1914 was when John W. Martin passed the Bar. How did a man with a fourth-grade education become a lawyer? You didn't have to go to high school, college, or law school back then. You just had to pass the exam. Ambitious to better himself, for years Martin studied at night and on Sundays. Becoming a lawyer boosted his innate confidence. In 1917, he was plucky enough to challenge multi-termed Mayor Bowden for his office.

Bowden was the movie industry's candidate. There were over 30 silent film companies in town, including Metro, which was later to become Metro-Goldwyn-Mayer. Martin was the candidate of citizens who didn't like all the hooliganism that accompanied the silver-screen crowd. Bowden claimed the tactics Martin used against him were a smear. Among other unsavory allegations, the young candidate charged that the mayor had used his office to profit his insurance business.

"I have never known of a candidate being successful who tried to force himself into office over the corpse of his opponent," Mayor Bowden complained.

Martin won by the biggest landslide in Jacksonville history, and the movie moguls read the voter's message as a warning to get out of town. They packed up and moved out West to Hollywood. At 32, Martin became the city's youngest chief executive.

Martin's local popularity grew during his three terms as mayor, and a new kind of Jacksonville emerged. When the city hosted the Southern Baptist Convention of 1922, the community mobilized to meet the needs of thousands of attendees. Hotels were jammed. *Welcome Baptists* signs were everywhere. It was the biggest convention Jacksonville had ever seen. Mayor Martin spoke to the massive crowd, and so did Governor Cary Hardee.

Once again the two feisty politicians were sharing the stage on Martin's inauguration day. A roaring battery of field artillery fired off a grand salute, as the retiring governor presented the new governor with the Great Seal of Florida. Seven short years later, Martin and Hardee would be trading insults in the 1932 gubernatorial primary. Hardee would accuse Martin of overspending and nepotism. Martin would claim Hardee had been a do-nothing governor, and he would claim to be running against "the three H's: "Hardee, Hell, and Hard Times." For now, however, on the steps of the Capitol at the supreme political event of his lifetime, future animosities between the two men seemed far away.

Governor Martin gave a very brief inaugural address. It was only 500 words and consisted mostly of platitudes. "The well-being and prosperity of the state can mean only happiness and benefits to the people," he said in a resonant voice that day. But none of the usual verve of his story-telling charm emerged during his speech. Jacksonville's *Florida Times-Union* described the entire ceremony as brief and simple "...as befitting a great Democratic State."

The highlight of the reception that evening was music played by the Jan Garber Orchestra. It was one of the hottest new jazz bands in the country. After orchestra members posed for a quick photo-op in front of a decorated railroad car bound for the inauguration, George Merrick, the millionaire developer of Coral Gables, paid to fly the musicians up to Tallahassee on a seaplane. Train travel was too slow for the band's tight schedule. They needed to hurry back the next day to continue their gig at the Coral Gables Country Club. Governor Martin specifically requested that the band play his favorite song: *When the Moon Shines in Coral Gables*. The song trumpeted up and down in a bouncy, washboard beat that made listeners of that era feel like hopping on the dance floor. Mrs. Martin was feeling somewhat better. She helped her husband host the party, but the couple left by 10 because of her fatigue.

D.P. Davis, the famous Tampa developer, was appointed a member of Governor Martin's private staff. At that moment in time, Davis was one of the boom's most sensational success stories. Only months before, his underwater lots in Tampa Bay sold out promptly on the day he offered them for sale. With contracts in hand, he started dredging and filling to make Davis Islands. Unfortunately, like so many boom-time deals of the era, his sales were not for cash. The prices were too high. He took back promissory notes on everything. Davis may have been a multi-millionaire, but most of his wealth was on paper.

Other members of the governor's official staff included developer Stockton Broome of Jacksonville and hotel magnate Charles B. Griner. The new governor became a vice-president and stockholder in Griner Hotels, Inc., a corporation which was set up to manage hotels around the state. Besides Griner, Broome and Martin, the new business venture included Thomas Meighan as one of its principals. Meighan was a top-billing movie star of that day. For actual day-to-day operations in the governor's office, Martin would come to rely heavily on his chief stenographer, Bessie Gibbs Porter, who continued to work for him for many years after he left office.

After inaugural festivities, Governor Martin got down to the business of keeping his campaign promises. First on the list was paving roads. Although the State Road Department had been in existence for nearly a decade, previous governors had not pressed bureaucrats to make road contractors carry out their assignments.

Private paving contracts were more lucrative, so road builders put public contracts on the back burner. During the campaign, Martin said he would clean house at the State Road Department:

"I will not hesitate to get rid of them and hang their political scalps out to dry on the Capitol door at Tallahassee, any more than a farmer would hesitate to hang out a coon skin to dry."

Martin quickly cleaned house at the State Road Department and put his friend, Fons Hathaway, in charge. At the beginning of 1925, only 898 miles of road had been built in the state's history. Even Dixie Highway, the route down to Miami, ground zero of the boom, was incomplete. Legions of Tin Lizzies had to negotiate sand, mud, and palmetto stumps on trails that were meant for horses and the big-wheeled buggies they pulled. By the time Martin left office in 1929, there were 2,975 miles of paved roads with 8,524 more miles designated for construction.

Governor Martin's other celebrated cause was providing free textbooks to students in Florida's elementary schools. Perhaps memory of his childhood poverty loomed large in his mind. A measure passed the legislature accomplishing that goal. In addition, Martin led an effort to amend the Florida Constitution to permit the state government to make direct appropriations to local schools. He personally sent out 15,000 letters to drum up support for that amendment.

By the end of his fifth month in office, he already had a county named after him. A group of ambitious investors in Stuart wanted to get in on the boom, but their county commissioners down in West Palm Beach were holding them back. Efforts to get the legislature to move on their request weren't getting any traction. Powerful Palm Beach County wouldn't let them break away to have a county of their own. St. Lucie County opposed them too, because a sliver of its hem was to be cut off as well.

The county secessionists raised $30,000 in "legislative sweetening"—an enormous sum for the times—but history has forgotten where they spent that cash. It wasn't enough to get the job done. Former Mayor Jackson B. McDonald was rumored to have pitched in a case of fine whiskey as a special gift to win the governor's attention. Names like *Inlet* and *Golden Gate* had fallen flat, but then Stuart Mayor John E. Taylor suggested that *Martin* "would make an awfully good name" for their new county.

The gambit worked. Governor Martin let it be known that he wanted his new county to breeze through the legislature. He made it clear that he thought the new county would be an important factor in the development of the East Coast of Florida. Opposition dissipated. The governor signed the bill creating Martin County on May 28, 1925. A confirmatory local referendum was held the following August.

The governor took more than just a passing interest in the county that put his name on the map. He appointed two of his former legal associates from Jacksonville to public office in Martin County: E.J. Smith became the county judge, and A.O. Kanner became state attorney. Within the year, the governor asked the people of Martin County to elevate A.O. Kanner to the office of state representative, and they complied. The governor's hotel corporation also took over management of the brand new Dixie-Pelican Hotel on the waterfront in downtown Stuart. Martin and his wife were the first guests.

A boom is a big illusion, a fever, a trance. A get-rich-quick epidemic spreads like the flu through the general population, but the symptoms frighten almost no one, until the delusion runs its course. At the first sign of trouble, gamblers double down like drunks taking another shot to chase away a hangover. During the summer of Martin's first year in office, some investors and opinion makers were beginning to sober up.

Unmistakable signs of the end began to appear, yet Governor Martin insisted that his state's real estate activities should not be called a boom; it was all just normal growing pains. Florida was finally reaching its potential, he explained. "The growth in Florida is phenomenal," he admitted, "but it is natural. There are 12 million people in the East who can come to Florida in the winter and eventually we hope to get most of them here."

There was so much construction going on in the corridor between Miami and Palm Beach, train tracks were getting clogged with carloads of building materials. It got so bad that the Florida East Coast Railway had to place an embargo on all shipments except perishables and necessities for human consumption. On top of that, speculators had been flipping property binders so many times that the final prices were too high for buyers at the bottom of the pyramid to pay. By September of 1925, Harold Keats of the Scripps-Howard newspaper chain had published articles nationwide proclaiming that the boom in Florida was over. Ohio bankers joined together to take out anti-Florida ads warning customers to keep their money at home.

Governor Martin launched a counter-offensive against a swelling tide of reality. He called together a dream team of Florida's biggest cheerleaders, and they held a press conference in New York City to tell Wall Street and the country the "truth about Florida." Martin declared that his state was the victim of fraud, and he asked reporters to help him stop the campaign of misrepresentations.

Men joining Martin for the public relations performance in the dining hall of the Waldorf-Astoria included Coral Gables developer George Merrick, railroad magnate S. Davies Warfield, developers Paris Singer and Baron Collier, Senator T. Coleman duPont, and a little known Daytona banker named David Sholtz. Sholtz would be John W. Martin's opponent in the run-off primary for governor in 1932. The emissaries left New York thinking they had put an end to detrimental propaganda against Florida. But in the words of one colorful observer of the times, "...the boom in Florida would be as dead as a salted mackerel three months later."

If the boom turned belly up shortly thereafter, not everyone could smell the stench. Governor Martin wrote in a preface to a book published in 1926 words to refute arguments about the end of Florida's prosperity:

"The sun of Florida's destiny has arisen, and only the malicious and the short-sighted contend or believe that it will ever set. Marvelous as is the wonder-story of Florida's recent achievements, these are but the heralds of the dawn."

The governor brought his cabinet to Stuart on January 28, 1926, for a belated celebration of Martin County's birth. A report in a local newspaper sounded a dissonant note 10 days before they arrived. It referred to a lack of real estate sales in the new county as "a holiday lull," and added that realty traders expected record sales to pick up soon. The report continued, "No one really believes that the bubble will burst, leaving Florida in the same condition as before."

When Governor Martin arrived, he reassured concerned boosters, whose life savings were invested in efforts to promote the new county. The adoring Martin County crowd lapped it up. Stuart's *South Florida Developer* described the governor's postprandial address in terms so glowing, it might have set the writer's pants on fire. "The address savored of those of Abraham Lincoln, through whose fun and anecdotes there was always the serious strain…"

A taste of Martin's allegedly Lincolnesque speech was recorded in the newspaper for posterity:

"Be not afraid of the propaganda against Florida that has been sweeping over the north… Why you might as well try to dip the St. Lucie River dry with a dipper as to stop the development of this great state. Whenever you see a man who is getting ahead of the crowd, you will hear all kinds of rumors against him."

When does positive thinking cross over the line into pathological denial of reality? When does it become fatal? George Merrick continued to pump all the millions he had made in Coral Gables back into grander developments. So did the Mizner brothers and D.P. Davis. In fact, almost all of Florida's big-time developers did, and the mom-and-pop developers and speculators followed their example.

Perhaps Walter Fuller, who lost millions in his developments in St. Petersburg, described it best: "We just ran out of suckers. That's all. We got all their money, then started trading with ourselves. Did I say we ran out of suckers? That isn't quite correct. We became the suckers."

If the long, slow crawl toward disaster through the first eight months of 1926 didn't dampen their perspective, the September hurricane should have. By today's standards, it might have been a Category 4. When it zeroed in on Miami just after midnight on September 18, the winds were strong enough to blow down most of the shoddy construction and break the dreams of thousands. George Merrick's quality construction withstood the test, but his gorgeous landscaping didn't. Neither did his sales. Headlines across the nation magnified South Florida's disaster.

Governor Martin's instincts led him to act immediately. As commander-in-chief of the state's militia, he rushed to the armory in St. Augustine and gathered the troops for an expedition down to the devastated area. On September 23, he arrived in Miami with the 124th Infantry. Miami's mayor, E.C. Rompf, met with Martin, and soon it was decided that martial law was not really needed after all. Business interests in the city were concerned about the bad publicity the storm had caused. They wanted to make sure people up North would not be frightened away from visiting in the upcoming winter season. Soon the head of the American Red Cross was making allegations that Governor Martin was blocking relief efforts.

"It is charged that Floridians are following the same tactics as those employed in the smallpox epidemic last winter, when every effort was made to minimize the news," the *New York Times* reported.

Martin shot back calling the charges "malicious and unjustifiable attacks made upon me for political purposes," and he blamed them on Ex-Governor James M. Cox of Ohio and his newspapers. Martin was developing a pattern of insinuating that malicious Northerners were out to ruin Florida's magnificent prosperity. Perhaps his Rebel roots were taking hold.

One of the governor's multi-millionaire supporters now knew the boom had been a big delusion after all. His many buyers wouldn't or couldn't honor their promises to pay off the notes for their purchases. D.P. Davis was rich on paper, but deeply in debt himself. He couldn't finish building his expanded archipelago project in Tampa Bay, or his new development in St. Augustine: Davis Shores. In that same month of October 1926, when Martin was embroiled in the aftermath of the hurricane and a storm of allegations in the national press, Davis boarded an ocean liner bound for Europe. He left his wife and took his girlfriend. Halfway across the ocean he mysteriously fell out of the porthole of his ritzy suite. His body was never found.

In January 1927, there was a respite from the gloom. Solomon Davies Warfield, the president of Seaboard Air Line Railroad, still believed that Florida would be making a comeback. Amid great fanfare and publicity, Governor Martin accompanied Warfield on one of Seaboard's Orange Blossom Specials, as that service was introduced to more cities around the state. It was a grand two-day event. Bands played and speeches were made at train stations along the route. An estimated 20,000 Floridians witnessed the combined events. For luxury trains of the time, the Orange Blossom Special could not be beat. It offered many frills, including a library, observation car, maid service, barbers and manicurists—not to mention stationery scented like an orange-blossom bouquet.

Warfield and Martin became great friends. Warfield invested heavily in Martin County and planned to turn its hamlet of Indiantown into a major city. He laid out streets and built the Seminole Inn in anticipation of an influx of new residents. His plans were still in the pipedream stage, when he suddenly passed away in October of 1927.

Three years into his term, with Davis and Warfield dead and so many other big supporters like Merrick financially destroyed, it was obvious that the state's economy had crashed. In the quiet darkness before dawn in the governor's mansion, Martin must have wondered what had hit him. Florida's bright heyday had looked so glorious in those early days when he rose to power. But the boom had burned out quicker than a Roman candle.

Perhaps it cheered the governor to bestow another great tribute to his memory. His monument might have lasted for centuries. Back in 1925, when the state seemed flush with cash, appropriations were made for a new building of neoclassical design in the Capitol complex in Tallahassee. When it opened in 1927, it was officially named the Martin Department Building. It housed government offices and the Museum of the State Geological Society, which displayed fossils, including a nearly-complete restoration of an American Mastodon. Only a few decades later, the building was demolished when the City of Tallahassee decided to replace it with its new City Hall. Demolition proved especially difficult. The Martin Building had been solidly built.

One incidental item from 1927 proved to be of more lasting significance. Governor Martin signed the bill making the mockingbird Florida's official state bird. He should be remembered when mockingbirds sing.

The year 1928 added to Martin's private misery. In the Democratic primary, he challenged incumbent U.S. Senator Park Trammell for his seat, but the race wasn't even close. On the campaign trail, he stressed his road-building record, but flocks of Northerners were no longer crowding onto the state's new highways. Those proud highways now led to boarded-up boomtowns. State Road Department Chairman Fons Hathaway, Martin's chosen successor to the governorship, also lost his primary. Doyle Carlton, the winner of the governor's race that year, claimed Hathaway mismanaged the funds and overspent. He alleged that road contracts didn't go to the lowest bidders.

If John W. Martin retained any illusions that Florida's renewed prosperity was just around the corner, they were blown away by another major hurricane. In September 1928, a devastating storm upturned the waters of Lake Okeechobee and poured them across the land, drowning nearly 2,000 people. Only the year before, Martin had pressed the legislature to authorize a 20 million dollar bond issue to beef up drainage operations, which might have provided better controls over the lake. The bonds were stalled in litigation.

Martin saw the bodies stacked up in Pahokee. The headiness of the gaudy mass-mania that had previously obscured his vision drained away as he looked upon the stunning quietness of the dead. Afterwards, he drove to Stuart to confer with his good friend A.O. Kanner. He made a $500 donation to the Martin County Chapter of the Red Cross at its headquarters on September 20.

"I could not see my own county suffer," the governor told the *South Florida Developer*. "I think more of Martin County than any other county in the state. No other county is so close to my heart as this one. I will not let the people of Martin County suffer."

He spent time in the area, revisiting Belle Glade, Pahokee, and Canal Point, and then on September 23, he gave a speech at the Red Cross headquarters in Stuart. His face was described as haggard.

"My heart is as heavy as any that beats in Florida tonight," the *Stuart Daily News* reported. "The world says good fellowship makes us one. Really—it is heartache that makes us one."

There were other difficulties with the job that placed a strain on the man. One time he signed four death warrants in a single day: two for murder; two for rape. Then he stood up from his desk and hurled the fountain pen out of the window.

The story of one man Martin ordered to die was, for a time, the subject of many sermons around the state. In 1927, a murderer named Jim Williams sat hooded in the electric chair, while his executioners argued over who had legal authority to pull the switch. Eventually, J.S. Blitch, the prison warden, called the governor to find out what to do. When asked, he said the man had been waiting to die for at least 15 minutes. That was too long for the governor. He commuted the sentence to life. Years later, Williams risked his life to save two visitors from being gored by a bull at the prison farm. For his courage, he was released.

A few months after the deadly hurricane there was another inauguration, but the cheers were not for Martin. Older, fatter, and more care-worn, he handed the Great Seal of Florida over to Doyle Carlton, a rival who had made the usual campaign allegations about the misdeeds of his predecessor. The bands played for Carlton, and the rapid rise and fall of John Wellborn Martin was set. He would never win public office again.

Martin ran for governor again in 1932, and the prize came so tantalizingly close he almost grasped it. Around the state, political pundits had him pegged as the front-runner. Only former Governor Cary Hardee was thought to stand in his way.

During the first primary, rivals took Martin down a notch. Charles M. Durrance, a state attorney from Jacksonville, had called him "*I* John," because he said Martin used the pronoun "I" more than any speaker of the English language. Durrance also told voters about Martin's tax certificate buying activities, including foreclosing on an 83-year-old woman in Pensacola and "a blind Negro mammy in Tallahassee." Durrance presented certified copies of Martin's legal proceedings to prove Martin was worse than Simon Legree. And Hardee drew blood when he complained about Martin spending so much on his Martin Building and giving state jobs to family members.

The hometown crowd in Stuart remained devoted to the man who gave them a county of their own. On May 31, 1932, the *Stuart Daily News* showed off its partisan zeal. "Martin County's own candidate will be here tomorrow night," the newspaper declared. "John W. Martin will be given such an ovation as never before has been seen in Flagler Park." Then the rhetoric of those *oompah* days went overboard: "John W. Martin is coming in all the glory of his manhood and with his glorious record as Florida's best Governor to squelch the lies that have been told about him…"

On June 2, the local headlines gushed: *Martin Replies to Critics with Brilliant Talk.* Martin defended himself by arguing that he built the Martin Building so the state wouldn't have to rent space anymore. He reminded voters that spending state money could be a good thing. Roads and free textbooks weren't the only presents he had given the people of Florida. He had modernized the penitentiary at Raiford, the state's mental hospital at Chattahoochee, and Florida's School for the Deaf and the Blind in St. Augustine.

In a field of seven, he came in first, but he had to contend with a run-off. A dark horse who had never held office came in second: Dave Sholtz. Martin was caught completely off guard. Believing the predictions of all the in-the-know politicos, he had prepared for a slugfest with Hardee in the anticipated run-off.

In round two of the primary, Sholtz railed about the "school book racket" and said the taxpayers had been overcharged for education. He complained about nepotism and politicians—"political racketeers," he called them, without naming his opponent's name—who wanted "to keep their hands in the gravy bowl." Sholtz insinuated someone had diverted tax money into the hands of his relatives. And he said he was sick of vicious attacks against his own character that were unbecoming even in a racketeer.

Sholtz's campaign against professional politicians and "profiteers" was really catching on. Martin's bland promise to make sure everyone would have "a dollar in his pocket and a smile on his face" was no match for memories of how he had presided over the stunning collapse of the land boom, which buried so many of the state's communities in debt.

Martin went negative—over-the-top negative. He tried to make Sholtz's Jewish ancestry an issue. Martin wasn't anti-Semitic himself. He couldn't have been. A.O. Kanner was one of his closest friends and advisors—and remained so all of his life. But Martin had to be hoping that a host of prejudiced voters would swing his way. Sholtz would only admit to being Episcopalian, so Martin presented affidavits to prove Sholtz was really a Jew. Even worse, there was a whisper campaign that Sholtz's wife had been arrested for prostitution one time in Jacksonville when she was young. Poor Alice Sholtz spent much of the next four years holed up in the governor's mansion avoiding the limelight.

Going negative backfired mightily. Florida's voters were not so low-brow as he had estimated. Martin lost the run-off primary by the biggest margin in history up to that time. Sholtz even out-polled him in his home county of Duval by two-to-one. Martin never ran for office again.

The campaign allegations Durrance made about Martin buying up tax certificates all over the state and foreclosing on people's homes were true. While all his millionaire supporters were losing their paper empires as the boom went bust, Martin saw an opportunity to make a fortune. He formed the Northern Investment Corporation—an odd name for a Southerner to choose. Located in Tallahassee, his corporation specialized in investments, bonds, stocks and mortgages. Although he had a law office in Jacksonville, Martin spent much of his time personally traveling the state picking and choosing distressed properties to buy. Bessie Gibbs Porter, or "Miss Bessie" as he called her, kept the books for the corporation in Tallahassee. She handled many of the details.

"If you don't mind out," Miss Bessie warned, "you'll have so many houses you can't keep track of them."

Martin traded some of his properties for profits, but he held on to most as rentals. By early 1937, he had nearly reached his goal of an income of a hundred dollars per day, which was a magnificent sum to collect in the depths of the Great Depression.

Martin became wealthy enough to buy a large tract of land not far from the State Capitol, where he went hunting. Hernando de Soto is believed to have set up winter camp at that location in 1539. Martin built an impressive brick lodge with stately columns. He called it Apalachee. It was a place for him to entertain the many friends he had retained. His primary residence was in Jacksonville, where he resided in a yellow brick mansion on the St. John's River in a posh section of Avondale.

Although he considered a bid for the U.S. Senate again in 1936, when Miss Bessie encouraged him to run, he decided his financial interests should take precedence. As he told her: "You know I have no way to make money now except trade, and that has really been my forte. I am no politician; I think I am a better trader or business man." Although he had a law office on the corner of Adams and Laura Streets in downtown Jacksonville, he must have only dabbled at the practice.

In 1941, a political plum was handed to him by a man he had appointed to the Florida Supreme Court back in 1925. Louie W. Strum, who was now a federal judge, appointed Martin to act as co-trustee of the Florida East Coast Railway. It was a handsome position he would hold for the rest of his life. Just like Henry M. Flagler, who had created the now bankrupt railway company, Martin could ride up and down the East Coast of Florida in his own private railway car. After the death of former U.S. Senator Scott Loftin in 1953, Martin became the sole trustee. He presided over the company's shift from steam locomotives to diesel.

In 1950, John W. Martin and his wife Lottie returned to Martin County for a celebration of the 25th anniversary of its creation. Not too much had changed since his last visit at the end of the boom. He and the county boosters had shared so many unrealized dreams. They had envisioned the county that bore his name would become one of Florida's major urban centers. Stuart, the county seat, was to be the most important port city south of Savannah. When he visited again in 1950, it was still barely more than a village. But Martin smiled and said how proud he was of the progress the local people had made. He rode in a 30-float parade with his old friend A.O. Kanner. An estimated crowd of 4,000 joined in the festivities.

Martin returned one last time to Martin County in January of 1958 to take part in ribbon-cutting ceremonies for a pair of new bridges to the beach. In what may have been the final speech of his life, he revealed a glimpse of the wisdom he had gained from the busted boom and his public rise and fall.

Florida." he said, "was built on hardships. Her banner flies high today, because of the courage of her people."

He told a small dinner crowd at the Sunrise Inn that evening that Martin County had always held a special place in his heart. Whenever he rode through in his private railroad car, he would put down his newspaper and look out the window. He said if he could be born again, he would like to be born in Martin County.

Three weeks later, Martin suffered a massive heart attack in St. Augustine, where his Florida East Coast Railway office was located. He lingered in a hospital for several weeks before dying on February 22, 1958, at the age of 73.

Martin was buried in a distant corner of Evergreen Cemetery, near downtown Jacksonville. In the midst of many marble and granite temples to the dead, his grave is marked by a small and unimposing stone. Beside it is the grave of his infant son, his only child. Lottie's grave is on the other side of their child's.

Quite often history is what happens to people and entire communities, while they are busy dreaming other dreams. Instead of a major urban center to rival communities up and down the coast, the county that bears Martin's name remains relatively unscathed by the over-development that spread across so many other parts of the state, because of people like him. For now, it still remains a relatively quiet retreat from the future shock imposed upon so much of our peninsula. And so, it is a place of irony.

Martin County owes its existence to the grand illusions of its local founders, who spent their time and personal fortunes trying to make it big. Most of all, the county owes its existence to a man who so wanted to be remembered by history that he put his name on the map. Perhaps someday, somewhere, somehow someone will take notice, and the man will get his wish.

A.O. Kanner, Evans Crary, Sr. (driving), John W. Martin, Lottie Pepper Martin, 1950.

A Tale of Two Judges

It was a tale of two judges—both born in West Palm Beach. The older circuit judge for Palm Beach County was a stellar jurist, wed to the proper application of law for more than 30 years. Higher courts rarely reversed his decisions. He was sober-minded, cool and lofty, humorless, but fair. In his court, justice was as sacred as a marble temple and just as solid. His name was Chillingworth. West Palm Beach's young municipal judge was highly ambitious, charming and friendly, but he wore a looming aura of disgrace. There were rumors of seamy indiscretions and friends in low places. His lifestyle was too lavish for his income. In his court, justice was a pliable commodity; he sold it like a broker. The young judge's name was Peel.

In the early 1950s, Judge Joseph A. Peel, Jr., teamed up with a lawman gone wrong. Floyd "Lucky" Holzapfel had once been a fingerprint expert for the Oklahoma City police, but now he was a jack-of-all-trades at the two-bit level of the underworld. Lucky sold get-out-of-jail-free cards for Judge Peel. Their "business" brought in lots of profits, because all the search warrants in the county were channeled through the young judge. It was easy money getting gambling operators and moonshine distributors to make monthly payments for protection from the police. Whenever the judge signed a warrant issued against one of his customers, the customer got a tip-off before the raid.

Judge Curtis E. Chillingworth sensed something unsavory about his young colleague on the bench. In those days a municipal judge could practice law on the side, and in 1953 Chillingworth formally reprimanded Peel for representing both sides in a divorce case. In 1955, Peel was caught committing malpractice again, and his case was set to come before Chillingworth. Peel was certain his upstanding adversary would disbar him this second time around, which would end more than his legal career. He planned on being governor of Florida someday, and a by-the-book ruling from Chillingworth stood in his way.

"It would ruin my career and our business," the young judge told Holzapfel.

Treachery was unloosed. Chillingworth and his wife, Marjorie, vanished after midnight on June 15, 1955. A massive manhunt ensued, but except for drops of Marjorie's blood on the wooden steps outside the Chillingworths' beach house in Manalapan, and except for footprints in the sand, no trace of the two was ever found. The killers left no fingerprints. For five long years a shocked community was left with the insecurity of unsolved mystery. And then one night Holzapfel got drunk enough to talk, and his drinking buddy called the police.

Holzapfel pleaded guilty to first degree murder. He was the state's star witness in the trial against Peel in March of 1961. He didn't even bother to bargain for a deal.

"People like us ain't fit to live," Holzapfel sobbed at his preliminary hearing. "We should be stamped out like cockroaches."

For 17 days (not including weekends) the trial took place in the old courthouse in Fort Pierce, as the window-unit air conditioners droned. Most of those March days were hot. The *New York Times* referred to our locale as part of the Deep South then. Most Floridians still sported a Southern drawl.

Jim Bishop, a newspaper columnist with Hearst's King Features Syndicate, attended the trial and described the courtroom in the old whitewashed courthouse in his book *The Murder Trial of Judge Peel* published by Simon & Shuster in 1962:

"On the second floor is the Ninth Judicial Circuit Court, a place with a high ceiling, wall stains, a condemned balcony where Negroes used to sit and watch white men adjudicate justice, a jury box, a lighted wall clock sponsored by a jeweler, an oil burner for chilly mornings, some council tables marked "St. Lucie County Property 201," and five rows of benches."

Judge D.C. Smith invited the press and dignitaries to take designated seats in his courtroom, and members of the public vied to make up the rest of the audience. The defendant, Joseph A. Peel, no longer a lawyer or a judge, flashed the full measure of his charm, and the affections of his pretty wife were daily on display. Who could have guessed that if the confident defendant beat his murder rap, he would face 160 charges of fraud in business dealings?

On the stand, two witnesses described the shocking end of the Chillingworths' lives. In addition to Holzapfel, Bobby Lincoln described the scene. He was a black pool hall owner and regular accomplice in Peel's judicial "business." Holzapfel said his buddy Peel had pointed out Chillingworth and had showed him the victim's beach house. Peel even knew what it looked like inside. He told Holzapfel what he and Lincoln had to do. According to trial testimony, Holzapfel and Lincoln followed the mastermind's plan, while Peel stayed home for an alibi.

The murderers arrived by boat and knocked on the door. Judge Chillingworth stood there in faded pink pajamas; his wife slipped into a robe. The hoodlums held them at gunpoint and bound their hands. On the way down the steps, Marjorie Chillingworth suddenly screamed. Holzapfel slammed a gun against her head and knocked her down. Judge Chillingworth unsuccessfully offered Lincoln money to spare their lives, and the victims were forced onto the boat. Then they chugged for two miles out to sea. The engine overheated and had to cool, over and over, drawing out the agony, as the good judge and his wife anticipated their incomprehensible fate.

When the boat stopped, Holzapfel wrapped a diving vest around the diminutive Mrs. Chillingworth and attached weights to it. He lifted her to drop her overboard.

"Honey, remember I love you," Judge Chillingworth cried.

"I love you, too," she said.

As she sank into the darkness, Judge Chillingworth jumped overboard. He was swimming with hands behind his back. Was he searching for Marjorie? Was he trying to get away? The flashlight found him, and the killers struck at his head with a shotgun. The shotgun broke in two. Still the judge swam, so Holzapfel steered the boat near enough for Lincoln to grab him and hold on. Holzapfel cut the anchor rope and tied it around the judge's neck. And then he dropped the anchor.

"Bobby let him go and he went down."

"Describe what you saw," State Attorney Phillip D. O'Connell said to Holzapfel.

"I saw the pink pajamas in the reflection from the light as he went down."

Judge Chillingworth was 58 when he was drowned. His wife was 56. On the night of the crime, Judge Peel was only 31.

Joe Peel seemed unfazed when he took the stand in his own defense. He flatly denied any involvement in the murders. He denied carrying on any type of bolita gambling operations or any other business with Holzapfel or Lincoln. He insinuated that the whole thing was a frame-up, because Holzapfel thought he was sleeping with his wife. On cross-examination, the defendant repeatedly denied asking the state attorney for immunity in exchange for giving testimony in the Chillingworth case. The state attorney was so frustrated by Peel's denial of the details of their previous conversation that he abruptly gave up asking questions.

Peel told a reporter afterwards he was confident he would win acquittal, or that the case would end with a hung jury. What he got was a conviction, but to the state's disappointment, it came with a recommendation of mercy. The sentence was life imprisonment. Peel escaped the electric chair.

Holzapfel spent the rest of his life behind bars. He died in 1996. Lincoln was given immunity for his testimony and never served time. He died in 2004. During the 18 years he spent in prison, Peel continued to deny involvement in the crime, until he made a deathbed confession to the *Miami Herald* in 1982. He was paroled nine days before he died of cancer. Just like the honorable Judge C.E. Chillingworth, Peel was only 58.

With my best wishes, I am

Sincerely yours,

The Vice President Who Became a Pirate

BRECKINRIDGE

There was an attempt to settle the Indian River region in the 1840s, but it failed. In the 1830s and 1850s small military outposts were built along the river, but they were abandoned. By the time Florida seceded from the Union on January 10, 1861, the Treasure Coast was practically as desolate as it had been when Florida first emerged from the sea to tangle herself in palmettos and flowering vines. And so, many miles of inhospitable shores remained uninhabited throughout the nation's internecine war. The best glimpses of that unpopulated time come through the eyes of travelers who took the time to write down their observations, two of whom were famous fugitives.

In June of 1865, six sunburned men jammed themselves together in an open boat so small, they couldn't lie down. It was a lifeboat stolen from a Union warship. Slowly they made their way down the vast sound known as the Indian River. The shores were treacherous then, especially during the steamy time of year. One of the fugitives complained that if you swung a bucket over your head twice, it would fill up with mosquitoes. Horse flies and sand flies tormented them, too. Even with both hands flailing, they still got chewed to pieces whenever they camped on shore, scavenged for edibles, or dug in the mud for drinking water. To sleep, they would bury themselves in the sand, exposing only their nostrils to the constant attack of bugs.

After the guns that raked a million men in the Civil War fell silent, John C. Breckinridge, the former vice president of the United States, still had to battle to survive. Northern newspapers were demanding the gallows for Breckinridge, who was now the Confederate States Secretary of War. Federal troops in hot pursuit had already captured nearly all the other members of Jefferson Davis' cabinet. The only hope for the Rebel warlord was to push through a no-man's-land of sub-tropical jungles, which included the Treasure Coast. He hoped to reach safety in the Bahamas, or maybe Cuba.

Brick-red from the sun and reeking in his unchanged clothes, you wouldn't have guessed Breckinridge was one of the most distinguished men in the country. Brutally handsome with shark-like eyes, he had been a popular national politician, who could stun any crowd with his powerful oratory. Just nine years prior, his party awarded him the nomination for vice president at the 1856 Democratic National Convention to balance the ticket headed by Pennsylvanian James Buchanan. When the duo affectionately known as "Buck and Breck" won the 1856 election, Breckinridge became the youngest vice president in American history. He was only 36. Unfortunately, within three weeks of the inauguration, he and the president had a bitter falling out. Like so many others in the North and South during those volatile years preceding the war, they found they could not get along.

Being at odds with President Buchanan did not diminish Breckinridge's stature. Kentucky elected him as its junior senator, and when the Democratic Party divided into factions during the nation-splitting election of 1860, he was nominated for president representing the Southern wing of the party. In fact, he came in second when he garnered six times more Electoral College votes than Stephen Douglas, the man history remembers as the big loser that year. The winner was Breckinridge's fellow native Kentuckian—his cousin's husband: Abraham Lincoln.

Although Breckinridge opposed secession until well after the war began, he ended up in gray. As a brigadier general for the South, he faced death on many fields, including Shiloh, Chickamauga, Chattanooga, and Cold Harbor. Then in early 1865, as the world began collapsing around the Old South's grand illusion, President Davis asked him to be the Confederacy's fifth and final Secretary of War. It was little better than an invitation to be hanged. Military leaders expected parole at the coming end of hostilities, but the top civilian leaders were facing trials for treason. Breckinridge accepted the position anyway. It gave him the power to tell his president "no." He used his office to squelch Jefferson Davis' plans to carry on a guerilla campaign for years.

"This has been a magnificent epic," Breckinridge said of the South's Lost Cause. "In God's name let it not terminate in a farce."

After Robert E. Lee's surrender at Appomattox, Breckinridge helped negotiate General Joseph Johnston's surrender to William Tecumseh Sherman in the foothills of North Carolina. At their conference, the Union General offered Breckinridge a bit of friendly advice: hightail it out of the country to avoid the rope.

Four of the passengers in the lifeboat didn't really have to flee. They were risking their lives to save their noble Secretary of War: two paroled Rebel soldiers; a colonel who had been his aide back in Richmond; and Tom Ferguson, Breckinridge's trusted slave. The other fugitive who faced the noose was Captain John Taylor Wood, a former professor at Annapolis—one of the most skillful navigators in the country. Although born in Minnesota, Wood had chosen the Southern side. To the North he was a pirate; to the South he was a dashing Confederate naval hero. During the war, he captured and sank well over two dozen U.S. merchant ships with his ironclad blockade runner: the *CSS Tallahassee*.

Captain Wood was a grandson of President Zachary Taylor, who— when he was a colonel— had challenged the Indians of the Treasure Coast region at the Battle of Okeechobee during the Second Seminole War. Wood was also a nephew of Jefferson Davis. In fact, he had been captured with the Confederate president near Irwinville, Georgia only a few weeks before; but he bribed a Yankee soldier to let him sneak into the swamp. Freedom cost him two of his gold pieces. Afterwards, Captain Wood met up with General Breckinridge at a designated safe house in Madison, Florida. A network of friends helped them through the inhabited parts of the state, but when they reached the Indian River's wilderness, they were on their own.

Captain Wood had spent years on the open sea, so he knew how to reckon their chances. The lifeboat rode too low to safely handle ocean waves, and they could never outrun the war ships in the Atlantic. But the Yankee steamers were unlikely to make any lengthy forays into the Indian River. It was much too clogged with shoals and sea grass for the big boats' hulls.

The Rebels' agonies were briefly relieved when they reached the site of present-day Vero Beach. The heavens opened up with a powerful downpour. The rain fell thicker than anything Breckinridge had ever seen. It was a chance to be washed clean and collect the first water in days that was truly drinkable.

The danger of capture increased as they neared the old inlet across from abandoned Fort Capron, several miles north of present-day Fort Pierce. A camp of Federal blockaders had gathered there. The fugitives spotted their pursuers' firelight on the shore. With muffled oars, they rowed past quietly in pitch-black darkness. And then they passed another old fort that had long since burned down—Fort Pierce—where General Sherman began his military career so many years before the Civil War. If Sherman had suggested their escape route through his old haunts, Breckinridge never told.

With the help of a military map made in 1856, the Rebels found an abandoned orange grove across from Herman's Bay. That's across the river from where the nuclear power plant looms today. A man named Philip Herman had homesteaded there many years before, when the luckless Indian River Colony was struggling to take hold. Settlers abandoned the area after a Seminole uprising. The Breckinridge party was disappointed to find that oranges were out of season, but they gathered lemons and a few coconuts for breakfast, which must have been the highlight of their trip through the Treasure Coast.

By then the weary Confederates could no longer tolerate the marshes, swamps, and tangles along the Indian River. In desperation, they decided they would rather risk dying at sea than be "sucked as dry as mummies" by the mosquitoes. They sailed off in search of Gilbert's Bar, an inlet on their map, which was slightly to the south of Stuart's present-day inlet. When they got there, the inlet was stopped up with too much sand, so, they headed south and lost themselves in a maze of winding water pathways in the Jupiter Narrows. Somewhere near Hobe Sound, the dunes separating them from the ocean became thin enough for them to drag the lifeboat across—and they rejoiced when they reached the blue water.

Sailing down the coast, they noticed black bears had been digging up turtle eggs. Following the bears' example, they dug enough eggs for a feast. Later, they found a band of Seminoles who had come to the coast to search for eggs, too. The Seminoles treated them to a fish dinner and then insisted on taking a big measure of their gunpowder in exchange for Coontie. Coontie was a type of flour the Indians made from dried taproots of the Arrowroot plant. Like cassava, if you don't process it correctly, it can kill you. But the Seminoles knew what they were doing. The flour was used to make unleavened bread, which Breckinridge described as thicker than pancakes, but "ten times as tough." Captain Wood said it was like chewing on *gutta percha* (rubber).

A Federal steamer spotted the fugitives on the shore. They scattered into the palmettos beyond the dunes, where mosquitoes began eating them alive again. With guns and swords drawn, a launch full of soldiers set out from the steamer. The Rebels decided they'd rather take their chances with the Yankees than surrender to the bugs again. When interrogated, they claimed they were just wreckers scavenging along the coast. Incredibly, the young Union officer in charge believed their lies. The Yankees traded tobacco for some of their turtle eggs before they let them go.

The powerful Gulf Stream wouldn't let the fugitives cross to the Bahamas, and it was obvious their dinky lifeboat couldn't sail to Cuba, either. That's why the man who had lingered a heartbeat from the presidency under crotchety, old James Buchanan suddenly became a pirate. By then, Breckinridge was a desperate shell of himself. He even looked like a pirate—unglamorously so— burnt to a crisp and standing there in rags and a floppy straw hat with his pistol drawn. South of Lake Worth, he and his fellow pirates-in-training came upon three men in a seaworthy sailboat. They took it at gunpoint; and they stole a bunch of their alleged victims' water, too, and some salted beef and crackers. But they gave the poor guys their leaky lifeboat and some turtle eggs—and a generous helping of Coontie.

After a brief gun battle with some real pirates who attacked them in Biscayne Bay, the Breckinridge gang agreed to a parley under a flag of truce. They bought a big jug of rum from them. But then, the gold-hungry pirates who sold them the rum tried to chase them down with a bigger sloop. Dodging canon blasts, the rum-soaked refugees from the Lost Confederacy pushed their much smaller sailboat over a reef and sailed to freedom on the open seas. If it hadn't been for the big storm in the Florida Straits, which sickened Tom so badly his master had to take over his servant duties, the last leg of the trip would have been happily uneventful.

In Cuba, the Breckinridge party was received by the governor with all the grand, luxurious attention normally afforded to state dignitaries. They were wined and dined and celebrated as heroes. Breckinridge gave interviews to the press. Even the *New York Herald* was delighted by his tale. The newspaper reported that his romantic and adventurous escape from Federal authorities would one day "form the groundwork of an exciting novel or thrilling drama."

Tom Ferguson, being a freed slave, was allowed to go home to Kentucky with the returning volunteers. Breckinridge didn't mind. Only Breckinridge and Captain Wood were on the *most wanted* list back home. Breckinridge moved to Ontario, where his wife and family joined him. Wood moved to Nova Scotia and settled down in a community of former Rebels. Breckinridge's wife couldn't take the icy winters in Canada, so they changed their exile to Europe for a time.

Eventually, the United States authorities forgot about the charge of treason.

So, in the end, John C. Breckinridge—Congressman, Senator, Vice President, U.S. presidential candidate, Southern Brigadier General, Secretary of War of the Confederate States of America, romantic pirate, and the biggest Rebel leader to set foot on the Treasure Coast— was allowed to return to live out his days in his hometown of Lexington, Kentucky. They put up a statue in his honor and received him as a favorite son.

The Discovery Of The Treasure Coast

Forget everything you ever learned about Juan Ponce de León. As it turns out, much of what we thought we knew is jumbled or untrue, or maybe just true enough to find a foothold for educated guesses. No doubt you've heard that modern historians are highly skeptical about the Fountain of Youth story. But did you know they can't agree on most things about our famous discoverer? They argue about his parentage, his birthplace, his birthday. There is no consensus on whether he was illegitimate, royal, or just a common stable boy. Some historians say he took part in Columbus' second voyage to the New World in 1493; others claim he arrived much later. For centuries they thought he discovered Florida in 1512; now they say it was in 1513. Worst of all, historians don't really know where Ponce de León landed when he first found our peninsula.

St. Augustine and Melbourne have asserted the loudest claims to bragging rights regarding landfall, but clearly the Nation's Oldest City has accumulated the most tourist revenues for the longest period of time in that regard. Henry Flagler even named his first luxury hotel in St. Augustine the Ponce de Leon when he opened it in 1888. Other attractions sprang up to make St. Augustine's claim official, at least from a business point of view. In 1923, when Florida was flush with land-boom hokum, a statue was erected to mark the spot where the great event took place—conveniently located right downtown near the tourist shops. Millions of visitors have seen it and believed, so the matter has been settled in the public mind.

But should it be? Well, not if you look at the evidence closely. Based on the only information historians have found, picking where Ponce de León made landfall is about as accurate as predicting where a hurricane will hit when it's five days out in the Atlantic. Our discoverer's landing took place somewhere on the eastern coast of Florida within a 300-mile range, give or take a few Spanish leagues, on April 3—or maybe April 2—1513. It wasn't even Easter Sunday like we've always been told. It was a week later. But out of the midst of all this baffling ambiguity some good news comes. The Treasure Coast is inside the cone of historic possibility.

Believe it or not, at least one historian concluded that Ponce de León first landed on our shores. His name was Louis D. Scisco, Ph.D., and he published his theory in a reputable, scientific journal. But that was 100 years ago, when almost nobody lived on the Treasure Coast, so no one got excited about the possibility. Locals probably never even heard about his theory. Scisco announced his research in an article published in a 1913 edition of the obscure *Bulletin of the American Geographical* Society. It was read by professional geographers nationwide, but not by the public at large. If Scisco's investigations had led him toward some popular tourist destination of that era, say Palm Beach, maybe the public might have heard about his research. But his calculations pointed to an overlooked stretch of desolate beach in what was then sparsely inhabited St. Lucie County. In 1913, no one cared.

In later years, a handful of historians appreciated Dr. Scisco's efforts. They used his arguments to come up with their own alternative locations for the first landing. They agreed that Ponce de León probably never sailed much farther north than the outskirts of Cape Canaveral, but Scisco calculated that the landing took place further south than those who cited his work. According to Scisco, Ponce de León first set eyes on the mainland just north of the original Indian River Inlet. That's about where the Navy Seal Museum is today; but he didn't drop anchor there. Before he landed, he sailed a few miles further north studying the lay of the land. He noticed some "cool woodlands" on a flat coastline, as described in the only recognized source document about the voyage. If Scisco was right, those inviting woods may have been forests of oaks in the neighborhood of Vero Beach. That could be the landing spot where Florida was officially discovered and named. Ponce de León disembarked and spent five days looking around. Was he looking for the Fountain of Youth?

It's too early to relocate St. Augustine's impertinently placed statue to Jaycee Park, but Scisco's argument does warrant consideration. First of all, you need to realize that all of Ponce de León's records of his trip were lost a long time ago. Nobody preserved the details of his voyage until more than 80 years after he discovered Florida—long after everyone involved was dead. That's when Antonio de Herrera, Spain's chief chronicler of the Americas, mentioned the discovery in his voluminous history, but he got the date wrong. It wasn't in 1512. Royal correspondence, since discovered, proves Ponce de León must have set sail in 1513. Herrera misstated the latitudes of known locations in the Bahamas, too. Scisco saw a consistent pattern in the erroneous data for Ponce de León's northwesterly journey from St. Germain near Puerto Rico. He recalculated the latitudes other historians have relied upon to take those errors into account. That's how he placed Ponce de León's landfall much further south on Florida's coast than previously imagined.

As further support for his theory, Scisco pointed to a map buried in the royal archives of Florence. It was drawn by a man named Ottomanno Freducci a year or two after Ponce de León's voyage. The map includes information corresponding to the first exploration of the coastline of Florida as reported by Herrera. Admittedly, the map is crudely sketched by modern standards, but frankly, most maps of that era look as if they were drawn by school children. Some look like Rorschach tests, and historians have imagined all kinds of geographical locations emerging from their blots and squiggles. Land masses are out of proportion, locations are inexact. But the Freducci map, in spite of its misalignments and perspectival challenges, clearly shows a coastline corresponding to the lower part of Florida.

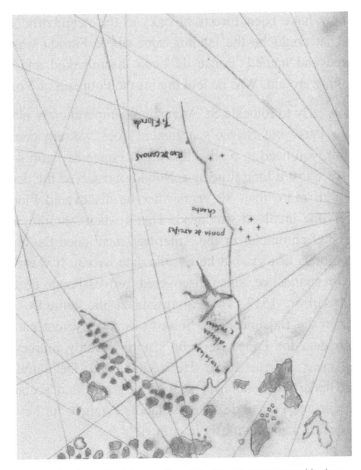

The Freducci map depicts a portion of Florida. Names are upside down.

The northernmost inlet shown on the Freducci map is called the Rio de Canoas [River of Canoes]. Keep in mind that most of the inlets we know today were artificially created relatively recently. In centuries past, what few inlets existed were shallow most of the time, and in some years were blocked altogether by sandbars. It took hurricanes and nor'easters to blow them open from time to time. Did the explorer name the uppermost inlet on the map River of Canoes because only small boats could navigate its shallow waters? If so, that certainly wouldn't describe the inviting harbor at St. Augustine that Pedro Menendez de Aviles made use of half a century after Ponce de León's discovery of Florida.

Scisco thought River of Canoes must have depicted the old Indian River Inlet, which was a small, winding tidal inlet. He also concluded that the water body shown further down on the map in the shape of a cross must represent Rio de la Cruz [River of the Cross], where Herrera reported that Ponce de León placed a cross hewn from stone. Scisco thought that must have been the Loxahatchee River. Others have thought it might be the St. Lucie River instead. Regardless of where it was placed, the stone cross of Ponce de León has never been found. Scisco theorized the jagged edges of coastline between River of Canoes and River of the Cross depicted Fort Capron Shoals and the shoals at Gilbert's Bar, which used to jut out into the sea. They are underwater now.

How do we find our way back through history when referenced landmarks are indistinct or washed away? What do we do when the records are all so scant? Why wasn't the discovery of Florida better preserved for posterity? Well, unlike Floridians of modern times, Juan Ponce de León's contemporaries did not think his accomplishment was all that special. The sad truth is that no clear record of his voyage was preserved because Spaniards thought it was a failure. Ponce de León didn't find anything he was looking for. He came back empty-handed: no gold, no boatloads of Indian slaves, no fertile lands—and certainly no barrels of water from an enchanted Fountain of Youth.

King Ferdinand II bestowed the coveted title of Adelantado upon him anyway, which made Ponce de León the ruler of the territory he found; but that honor must have felt like a consolation prize. Like all conquistadors, he longed for fame and tremendous fortune. He wanted glory. Florida earned him none of that. While other conquistadors brought back fleets of silver and gold from Mexico and South America, making Spain the richest and most powerful nation in the Old World, he must have felt like he had become the *Adelantado of Nada*. Even Ponce de León would be surprised to find us celebrating his "achievement" 500 years later.

His Florida adventure cost him plenty. Under the terms of the contract he signed with King Ferdinand II, Ponce de León was responsible for covering all the expenses of his unsuccessful expedition. He equipped three ships with provisions and crew. He hired Antón de Alaminos, the most experienced navigator in the Caribbean, who had helped Columbus find his way. Alaminos's wages couldn't have been cheap. Although it took only about four weeks to find the Florida coast, they spent six or seven months exploring.

If he hadn't been so restless, Ponce de León might have stayed down on the farm in a province of Hispañola with the innkeeper's daughter he married. Of course, none of us would have ever heard of him if he'd been content to live at home. In his younger years on his plantation, he grew wealthy marketing cassava bread. Spanish ships stocked up on cassava for their voyages back across the ocean, because it remained edible for months. But managing his Indian slaves from the comfort of a big stone house in Higuey had not been enough to quell his Adelantado-size ambition. When offered, he jumped at an opportunity to become governor of Puerto Rico, where he enslaved the natives to mine for gold. But Columbus's son, Diego, sued and won control of Puerto Rico, because his father saw that island first.

That's when Ponce de León worked out his deal with the king. If he found someplace new, the king said, he could be the ruler there. That's how he ended up finding Florida. But when the deal was over, he had nothing to show for spending his fortune, risking his life, rolling around on the sea. It took a long time for him to replenish his finances. Then eight years later in 1521, he returned to the Gulf Coast of Florida with a small flotilla intending to establish a settlement. But he was promptly hit in the leg with an arrow shot from the bow of a hostile native, and he retreated. He died when he reached Havana. For 300 years afterward, the Spanish lost men and money on their Florida investments. That's why they gave it away.

Without the Fountain of Youth story, Juan Ponce de León might only be remembered as Florida's first failed developer. In a land where bigger-than-life land booms have been followed by busted dreams over and over again, he could be the patron saint of hard-luck schemers. That's why the Fountain of Youth part of the story is too important to just let go. Maybe hardboiled realists can't believe our hero was a romantic fool, but his quixotic quest is the only thing that makes him endearing. It touches the impossible dreamer in all of us.

The story's charm is probably a big reason why we've always ignored the inconvenient truth that other explorers like Cabot, and possibly Vespucci, probably saw Florida first. Not to mention that one of the Indians Ponce de León met on Florida's Gulf Coast in 1513 already spoke Spanish. When it comes to discovery, historians have ignored the non-Europeans, who traveled back and forth from the islands—the ones who helped our "official" discoverer find his way. But let's give credit where credit is due. Ponce de León was the explorer who changed the name of the place to Florida. Before that, the natives of the Caribbean called it Cautió, or Chantio, which the Spanish historian Herrera said was an Indian word for the palm-plaited thongs the original peninsular natives wore.

When you think about it, why wouldn't an aging, sunbaked conquistador have believed in the possibility of waters that could restore a person's youth? In 1513, science was in its infancy and many of its practitioners were alchemists, who were busy looking for ways to turn ordinary metals into gold. The widespread skepticism and disenchantment of the modern world was centuries away. The human mind was still ensconced in wonder. Stars were thought to control men's destinies, and black magic was a force to be put down. All over Europe, church and crown were still trying to rid the world of witches. Another conquistador, Coronado, rode off in search of the mythical Seven Cities of Gold. So, why should we have to stop believing Don Juan Ponce de León actually hoped to find waters that might bring eternal youth?

Peter Martyr, a contemporary of Ponce de León, was an official historian with access to the Spanish king. He wrote the Pope a letter about rumors of an island far to the northwest of Hispañola, where the waters of a continual spring had the power to make old men young again. The rumor had spread through the court, he said, and many people of wisdom and fortune believed it to be true. Did that include the king? Herrera, who wrote the celebrated source document about the voyage, also said that in addition to other purposes, Ponce de León "...went to seek the fountain of Bimini, and in Florida a river, giving credence in this to the Indians of Cuba, and others of Española, who said that bathing one's self in it, or in the fountain, old men would be turned into youths." Hernando de Escanlante Fontaneda, a shipwreck survivor who spent 17 years as a slave of the Florida natives, confirmed the Indians' steadfast belief in the existence of magic waters. In his memoirs from 1575, he wrote that he was forced to roam with them all over the peninsula compulsively bathing in every river, brook, lake and swamp without success. And Fontaneda stated categorically that Ponce de León had searched for the rejuvenating water, too. Perhaps he learned that from his captors.

Those who dismiss Ponce de León's fabulous quest have to close their eyes to the records we have. For the rest of us, the story enhances and embellishes the fun of knowing things about a world that is often illogical. Facts aren't always drab. The magic of the place he called Florida derives from an allure of eternal youth, which is, after all, a bold and winning attitude of mind enwrapped in illusions of timelessness. Why would anyone not want to assume our Founder had it, too?

Thomas Moran, a famous landscape artist of the Hudson River School, understood the aesthetic appeal of the Ponce de León story. He drank it in when he visited St. Augustine with his wife in 1877 in the midst of a Fountain of Youth tourist craze. The result of the inspiration he took away with him was perhaps the most majestic 19th century painting with a Florida theme: *Ponce de León in Florida*. Moran superbly blended reality with romance to create that deeper experience all great art achieves. Although Moran hoped his 5 by 9-foot painting might hang in the Capitol Building in Washington, Henry Flagler bought it to adorn his Ponce de Leon Hotel. Later, Flagler moved it to Whitehall, his marble palace in Palm Beach. Today you can find Moran's impressive painting at the Cummer Museum of Arts and Gardens in Jacksonville.

Ponce de León never knew the treasure he had found in Florida, or the metaphor his life bestowed. History overlooked his achievement for literally hundreds of years, until the tourists came. Now, a more skeptical age attempts to overlook the enchantment of his adventure. But as we celebrate the fifth centennial of Ponce de León's contribution to the world, the truth cannot be blotted out entirely: Florida was indeed founded on a fantasy, and fantasy has always been a prime ingredient for making Earth a paradise. It was, in the end, a truly magnificent discovery. And quite fittingly, Florida remains a place for the young, and the would-be young, and all the young at heart.

For as long as history lingers in a state of disarray, communities from the First Coast down to the Treasure Coast and all points in between can claim our discoverer for their own. But someday in some long-forgotten recess of a darkened archive, a crumbling logbook may be dusted off and transcribed. And if Dr. Louis D. Scisco's supposition turns out to be correct, then an unnoticed spot on the overlooked Treasure Coast will finally come to light. That's when the world will learn anew where American history really began. The blank spaces in history's vaunted volumes are often filled with rumors, legends, and myths. Surprisingly, in the case of Ponce de León, the myth is not as we suspected—that he searched far and wide to find an illusion we all might hope were true. The myth is where he landed.

Old Times There Are Not Forgotten

"She's a reee-ahl faaahr-cracker," Joe Keller said to me in his long, drawn-out Kentucky brogue. He was describing my grandmother, Talley McKewn Crary.

Way back in 1980, Joe and I were seated side-by-side at the wedding rehearsal dinner for his brother, Mike, and my sister, Robin. We were listening to my grandmother, who was busy entertaining a table full of guests at the old lodge nestled in the woods in Pennyrile State Park in Kentucky. A few minutes earlier, Talley had launched into one of those animated performances with which she enlivened every gathering graced by her presence.

Although you had to drag her to any social event, as soon as she arrived a light would flash on in her blue eyes—and the show would begin. She had some favorite comments and vignettes that she frequently drew from her stock-in-trade, but she was not overly repetitious. Most of her material was fresh, but even her old stories continued to be entertaining, because they were just so good, and because her delivery was flawless. Joe was laughing at one of her favorite tales about a breakfast she shared with one of my cousins when he was a little boy.

"One time we had taken my oldest grandson, Larry, to the mountains," Talley said. "He was about six years old at that time. We first went by South Carolina and stayed there a couple of days, and then we went on to North Carolina to see the mountains. And he was—oh—excited to death, and we had a wonderful time. One morning on the way back home—we were at someplace in Georgia—it was Dublin, I think—and we went in this restaurant to have breakfast.

Larry, as I said, was six, and he had just learned to read. So—we ordered our meal which was grits, and country ham, and eggs. The waitress wrote down grits, country ham, and eggs. And then she dittoed the three other orders. And we ate our breakfast, and when she brought the bill, Larry said—he called me *Bammer* back then—he said, 'Bammer, can I see it?' And I said, 'Yes!' So he got it and stood up, and he read, 'One grits, country ham, eggs—one little prick, little prick, little prick—one little prick, little prick, little prick—one little prick, little prick, little prick. Bammer! Who ate all the little pricks?' Well, of course the restaurant was filled with men, and they just died laughing—and we got out of there in a hurry!"

As always, her audience erupted into laughter at the end of that story, even those of us who had heard it many times before. So many elderly women of her generation seemed handicapped by a stern and prudish disposition, which leaves company feeling ill-at-ease, but this fine Southern lady could always break the ice with an unexpected declaration—often bordering on risqué.

"When I was a young girl," she said from time to time, "I was half afraid the white slavers would get me, and half afraid they wouldn't."

New acquaintances were caught off guard by such confessions, because something about Talley seemed positively Victorian. She was so prim and proper and mannerly, and yet she poked fun at the formalities to which she professed allegiance, as if to get even with social conventions that restrained her.

"I've always been a rebel," she'd announce, excusing herself whenever she felt she may have taken a step or two beyond the border of propriety.

To new brides, including my own, she gave the same words of insightful advice. "To be a good wife, you have to be a cook in the kitchen, a lady in the parlor, and a hussy in the bedroom!" With such counsel coming from a fine lady in her 80s and then 90s, listeners could draw the conclusion that maybe the days of long ago had not been quite as drab as so many other elders made them sound.

Talley was truly the life of every party she attended. Visits to her house at 311 Cardinal Way in Stuart, Florida, or her small cabin in North Carolina, were turned into parties, too. She was a great master of the fine art of conversation, because she understood that conversation is a team sport. Everyone present needs to be a participant, no matter how inept they feel. She knew how to make even the dullest company appear to shine and feel good about themselves. A lackluster comment from a guest was warmly received by her with encouraging delight. She would laugh with melodious glee whenever one of her guests said something halfway humorous.

Talley seemed to want to inspire the world to get on with the business of making social occasions more fun. But few of us could be so entertaining, and so it always fell to her to take center stage. Oh, and she knew precisely how to enchant her listeners with her intriguing stories, slightly naughty jokes, and those insightful snippets of wisdom, which peppered her conversations. Only the most careful listeners could pick up on the more prickly points of her dialogue, which she always buried under a generous covering of humor.

She had plenty of practice entertaining. For 40 years, Talley had been the wife of a public man, who became a prominent politician in Florida.

"I always have despised politics," my grandmother said on many occasions. "And wouldn't you know it—I'd marry someone who liked it."

Her husband, Evans Crary, Sr., spent 18 years in the Florida Legislature. At the pinnacle of his career in 1945, he became Speaker of the House, and afterwards, he became a state senator. There were countless cocktail parties, political receptions, and dinners at the governor's mansion. A politician's wife must always be on stage. Talley loved all the "trappings" of politics, as she called them, but she despised the campaigns and what it took to gain office. Like so many other aspects of her life, she had a kind of love-hate relationship with the political world and all of its attendant deceptions.

In her day, the wives of most of the state's political leaders stayed behind at home, but not Talley. She frequently boasted of her decision to leave her sons behind with her mother and spinster sister so she could accompany her husband to all the legislative sessions. She served as his secretary for a salary of six dollars a day. She often said when she first went up to Tallahassee, she took one look at all the fancy girls lined up in the Capitol Building waiting to entertain the legislators, and she knew she couldn't leave her husband unattended. He was hers, she proclaimed, and she didn't plan on sharing him. With a wife as entertaining and as memorable as Talley, it's no wonder Evans' political star rose quickly.

"It was really exciting, but I was terrified," she said of her first encounter with Tallahassee society. "You know, all my life I have really lived in somewhat of an anxious and fearful state—always hoping that I would do good and fearful that I wouldn't. And I *dreaded* meeting people. I was very shy. Nobody believes it, but I was and still am to some extent."

No one has ever seemed less shy than Talley Crary. She masked her shyness with the best bluff anyone ever mounted. Every crowd became her audience. Spectators succumbed to her charm and wit. Clearly, she belonged on stage. Whenever she lost herself in her role, and folks were eating out of her hand, you could tell by the fire of delight in her eyes, she was really enjoying herself and her memories of days gone by. And yet, she still protested.

"I hated Stuart," Talley sometimes confessed to disbelieving visitors. "I had never lived in a small town like this where everybody knew everybody else's business and talked about it. And Evans finally getting into politics, I had to be somewhat like Caesar's wife—above reproach, and I wasn't constituted that way. If I wanted to do something, I did it, which, of course, would bring the house of cards down on my head every time."

A winter resident Evans represented let them occupy his house on the river during their first summer together in Stuart. The sand flies were unbearable at night. People didn't have air conditioning in those days, so they had to keep the windows open. They rubbed the screens with crankcase oil to try to hold the sand flies at bay. Talley remembered her first months with Evans as miserably hot, buggy, and smelly. Downtown, all the stores were filled with smoke. Everybody burned Bee Brand insect repellent in a futile effort to chase mosquitoes away.

"And if you ordered a sundae," she said with a look of feigned disgust, "it would taste like Bee Brand insect repellent."

"I can tell you're not from around here," one crusty old guy in the grocery store said to her when she first moved to Martin County.

"How's that?"

"Cuz you swat 'em," he said of the mosquitoes. "Most folks 'round here just *bresh* 'em off."

Even her heartfelt grievances did not feel like real complaints. They were sugared with doses of humor that danced to the tune of her happy voice. She always lifted the spirits of her company.

Of all the descriptions I've heard of my grandmother's social persona, I think Joe Keller's was the one that really hit the mark. Talley was indeed "a real firecracker"—in public. But as all great performers know, there is a life behind the scenes. Talley was not just a one-, two-, or even three-dimensional personality. She was a tangle of complexities which, at times, even she could not unravel. Solicitous to her stellar reputation to a fault, she kept her world behind the scenes almost entirely private. For Talley, being in the presence of others was nearly always synonymous with acting—but a part of her grew so weary of the show.

"Oh, good Godfrey, who is that?" she'd cry out whenever she heard someone pulling up in her driveway. But as she was complaining that she wasn't in the mood for another round of company, she was automatically patting the curls of her gray-and-white hair to make sure they were all in place. Moments later a carload of visitors would enter her TV room, where they were hospitably entertained. Sometimes everyone would move out to the cushier furniture in the living room, a place she called her *parlor*. Even when her guests stayed long beyond their welcome, she never seemed to tire.

Talley always wanted to live in a perfect world. It was a world embellished by the romantic traditions of the Old South. As she entertained you with her Scarlet O'Hara charm, she would draw you into that world and make you believe in the forgotten splendor of days that have long since gone with the wind. I lived in that world when I was a little boy. In part, I am almost certain Talley helped me learn how to run away to that more beautiful realm, where the ugliness of the ordinary world cannot claim you for its own.

Of course, I believed in my grandmother's ideals, and I assumed they were nurtured in the idyllic settings of her childhood. When I was young, I imagined she had lived in some Garden of Eden the modern world destroyed before I was born. I joined with her in lamenting its passing, and I was homesick for a place I had known only in our shared imagination.

Every now and then Talley would make statements that seemed out of place with the picture I'd acquired of our perfect past. The first, as I recall, was when she told me, "When I was a little girl, I used to hide in a corner of the house and read." She said she would always run away into her books. She said she told herself when she was a child that she must have been adopted or kidnapped by the McKewns. Surely, she couldn't have been a member of their family. They were so different from her, she told me. I began to wonder about thorns in the rosebushes of our perfect garden, but my probing questions elicited few details and no clear explanations.

Over the years we talked many times about family history—about her recollections. I really thought she had told me practically everything she could remember, but less than two years before her death, she surprised me with new revelations about her father, William Talley McKewn.

I had long known that when my grandmother was 14, she and her family moved into my grandfather's neighborhood in Tampa. Their new house was just two doors down from 14-year-old Evans Crary and his parents. Once in a long while, Talley would tell me that the Crarys looked down on the McKewns, but she wouldn't say why. Her future mother-in-law became her lifelong nemesis. They couldn't stand each other. But Alice was the daughter of a backwoods stagecoach driver and she met my orphaned great-grandfather Perley Frederick Crary at a boarding house where she was working as a waitress. How could she have felt so uppity? For years I couldn't solve the mystery of what Alice found so distasteful about Talley's family. I pressed to learn the answer one more time.

"How could she have possibly looked down on the McKewns?" I asked.

"Well," my grandmother said with a sigh of resignation. "My father was a gambler. He played cards all the time, and sometimes he wouldn't come home. And we'd worry that he might have lost his paycheck again. And how would we eat? Well—he won that last house we lived in. He won it in a game of cards. The man who lost the house—well, his son lived there. And Daddy evicted him with a crowbar. We were sitting in the car, and Mother screamed, 'My God, don't kill him!' And we thought Daddy was going to kill him, but he moved out, and we moved in."

With such a violent stir, I could finally understand why the neighbors might have gotten a bad impression of the new Irish family on the block. The incident also sheds light on why Talley sometimes said she wanted to run away from reality when she was a girl. Her favorite grandfather—the one she loved—had a plantation in South Carolina. Whether it was half as grand as Tara in *Gone With the Wind*, or whether it was just a big farm in the middle of nowhere, it always seemed so much better than home. The old Confederate veteran John Henry Dukes—she called him Papa—wore an air of nobility she craved. Maybe it was the way he sat at the top of those tall steps, as his sharecroppers bowed before him on payday. He allowed Talley to hand them the money. My grandmother always belonged to that plantation and its imagined ambience of regal antebellum days.

In stark contrast, however, her other grandfather, George R. McKewn, had no redeeming qualities in her eyes. To her, he was one of those property-less whites, who fought the War Between the States until the day he died. She remembered him as the ne'er-do-well grouch, who came with his humorless, priggish wife—Mamie Steadman McKewn—to spend long months with her family in Florida, and spoil her fun. Crippled in battle by a minié ball that shattered his knee, bitter and unforgiving, she found the old Rebel's crassness embarrassing. He interrogated every one of her friends to make certain they had no Yankee blood. If they did, they couldn't come in the house. She openly made her detestation for him known. In fact, she was forbidden to attend his funeral when she was 11, because she boldly announced to her parents that she intended to dance on the dead man's grave.

Along with her maternal grandfather, her mother Maggie Dukes McKewn was a veritable saint—an icon of all the greater virtues of womanhood—or so my grandmother presented her to me, ever since I was old enough for memory to attach itself to consciousness. It was not until sometime shortly before I conducted my second taped interview with Talley and her sister Sophie that I learned of her mother's secret flaw, which so troubled my grandmother all of her life. It was then she told me of the day that she and Sophie were rummaging through their attic. They were teenagers then. In a box they found a letter. It was from their father to their mother. In it, he wrote how he would always love their eldest sister, Syril, as if she were his own child.

Well, I was as shocked as they must have been when they first learned the news! Their sister was a child of another man! Who was her father? Talley claimed to know so little, but Aunt Sophie turned out to know much more. For all of their lives, neither daughter ever discussed the matter with their mother, but Sophie learned the secrets from Aunt Pearl, one of their mother's sisters.

Talley tried very hard to believe her mother must have been married to Syril's father, but Sophie insisted that was not the case. Both told me the tale of a handsome traveling tombstone salesman named Brown, who came through Orangeburg, South Carolina. All the girls wanted him, but Maggie turned his eye. Contrary to her parents' admonitions, Maggie ran away with him and came home pregnant.

"He beat her," Sophie told me one time.

How long she was away from home with Brown was never clear. Sophie said Brown turned out to be married. His misdeeds did not sit well with the family. After Maggie returned to have her child at home, Mr. Brown met with an untimely death. According to family legend, his bones lie "at the bottom of a millpond"—or so Maggie's brothers said. Did their father investigate his disappearance? He was, after all, the Sheriff of Orangeburg County. That dark secret troubled Talley all her life.

There was never any need to think that Maggie's past disqualified her for sainthood. King David had the murder of Uriah and his illicit relationship with Bathsheba to plague his conscience. Maggie Dukes had Brown. But unlike so many, whose checkered pasts incite them to point a prosecutorial finger at motes in other people's eyes, Maggie was always understanding of her fellow human beings' failings. She displayed those humbler qualities Jesus told us we should have. She never judged anyone harshly. Even the most open sinner was excused with a phrase our family remembered her saying so very often: "He means well."

When 12-year-old Syril appeared to be dying with scarlet fever, Maggie bargained with God. "If you let her live, I will never complain about my daughter again." Well—Syril lived, and Maggie kept her pledge, although she certainly was tested for her bargain. Beautiful Syril, cold and cruel, went half-mad sometimes with anger. She would cuss her mother up and down, but Maggie would just look out a window and sing a hymn and smile. So I was told, and I can believe it, because I well remember my great-grandmother's beatific smile. It was always on her face whenever I saw her.

There were many unpleasant details about life, which didn't fit into my grandmother's perfect world. But she always fell back upon that distant vision of Papa's place in South Carolina, which never ceased to appear ideal. Sometimes I have wondered if that faraway world was ever real. Was it ever more than early morning carriage rides with Papa through the cotton fields in the bottom land to the well-swept yards of the Negro hands? Was it more than the sweet, delicious taste of the scuppernong grapes—white and black—in the arbors along the way from the main house? Was there something else to fill the days besides her endless playing in unhorsed wagons?

The details of that distant splendor now seem scant as I review my notes and tapes and memory. I have stood in Orangeburg on a summer day a few short years ago and tried to see the glory of the past, but the present of the place did not lend itself to that greater beauty we hold in unexamined dreams. It was hard for me to see the magic of the setting. To find it once again, I had to hearken to my own brief childhood memories of the place.

In May of 1968, my cousin Larry and I joined our fathers and grandmother on a trip to Orangeburg to attend my great-grandmother's funeral. A grave was dug for Maggie Dukes McKewn beside the resting place where her husband had been interred since 1922. I was

13 years old and not so grown up as I imagined. The solemnity of the mournful occasion did not rub off on me. Instead, I soaked in the aura of a sleepy Southern town whose existence had mingled with dreams my grandmother lent to me. Papa Dukes' plantation was no longer there for me to see firsthand. The house and cotton fields had long since disappeared, but something about that vanished world still lingered on the edges of my understanding.

We stayed in Mildred Wannamaker's house, which was, to me, the finest house in which I had ever spent the night. Maybe it was just an ordinary two-story brick house in an ordinary Southern town—I can't remember enough facts to be objective now—but it seemed so much finer than anything I had ever seen back home. It was full of fine furnishings and enchanting bric-a-brac you could not touch. Outside, Cousin Larry and I played catch, while the grown-ups took care of grown-up things inside. That evening we were invited to join the conversation in a cozy, wood-paneled room, where we ate Chipsters— a packaged potato snack—and we laughed about old times the grown- ups told us about.

In the morning, the wonderful aroma of breakfast reached me in my upstairs room where I lay ensconced in the cushy luxury of satiny sheets in a big four-poster, canopied bed. The aroma quickly drew Larry and me down to the dining room, where a chatty black maid was setting out a spread of food on silver platters glistening in an ornate dining room. For all of my life, it has seemed to me to have been the finest breakfast I ever had. It was the essence of the culture I had nursed upon in my dreams of antebellum days. The steak sausages with gravy, and the cheese grits, and eggs, and smoky bacon I feasted on have never tasted better.

After breakfast we dressed in our finest clothes and went to the funeral at an old Methodist church. There had been riots in Orangeburg. It was part of the unrest which had taken hold of our homeland as it wrested itself away from the grip of Old South illusions. On the way to the church, I remember seeing three large wreaths in a park, and I was told they stood at the place where three young African-Americans had been killed in a civil disturbance. For a moment I felt some indescribable sense of fear and alienation in the presence of those temporal monuments to early death. I did not understand the notion of civil rights at the time or why our world was crashing down. The funeral service for my great-grandmother did not burn itself as deeply into my memory as those wreaths. Of that service, I have only the vaguest recollection of a droning voice emanating from a distant pulpit and my efforts to sit still and stay awake.

Afterwards, we gathered at the cemetery beside a tall obelisk bearing the name of *Dukes*—the largest monument in a quiet field of tombstones. It bore witness to Talley's claims to family prominence in the town where she was born way back in 1905. Years later I would return to read the inscriptions, but at that time I could barely be bothered, nor did the graveside ceremony command my attention.

Larry and I were permitted to wander away to be the young boys we were. We played in the small forest a few hundred feet away, hunting about for treasures and throwing bits of dried clay at a fallen tree. And that was all—some idle hours in an idle town—but it seemed to be so much more, because it offered a brief respite from school and troubles at home. It is by such distant analogies that we experience another person's world. And now it makes me think that maybe I saw—if only just for a moment—the special place where my grandmother always lived in her imagination.

A month before that day in Orangeburg, my grandmother's brightest hopes had ended. My grandfather died. Talley worshiped Evans, and when he was gone, she worshiped his memory even more. In the spring of 1968, he had lingered in a hospital bed at home for weeks while cancer marched through his body doing its killing business.

On the night he stopped breathing, we got a call at my home in Stuart, and my father and I rushed over to my grandparents' home on nearby Cardinal Way. I was pointedly instructed not to look in the TV room, but of course, when Dad and Grandmother were distracted by their conversation, I walked to the door and peered inside. It was a frightening scene for me to gaze at the breathless body of my grandfather, but I understood he had finally found peace from his months of suffering.

Talley could not bear the thought of spending that night alone, and whether I volunteered or my father directed me to spend the night, I can't recall. But I so clearly remember the long hours in the dark, where the faint light of the moon or a nightlight reached us, as my grandmother sobbed and gasped. All I could think to do was to pat her back, but it was little comfort for a wonderful woman in so much agony. In the morning, sunlight brought no promise of happiness to come.

For four of five dark years, my grandmother rarely consented to be cheery. But sometime after her sister, Sophie, moved into Talley's home to relieve the loneliness, she began to reacquire the cheerful face she put on for the world. Then she was her old, entertaining self almost all of the time.

Talley never remarried, although she would have made an elderly man a wonderful bride. As the years went by, she retained a hardy youthfulness and seemed to grow more beautiful. Once, on a boating trip to Mexico with her longtime friend Frances Langford, Talley had a wonderful time with a widower—I think she said his name was Harry. But she felt too guilty for her fun and would not hear of suggestions to continue any such companionship. Her mother bore her widowhood for 46 years, and Talley endured hers for 34.

Sophie moved in with her sister sometime in June of 1972, and the two of them became such a famous pair that their names blended into one. It was always Grandmom-and-Sophie, or Talley-and-Sophie, or Mimi-and-So. How could anyone imagine them apart? And yet, there was a mild tension underlying their relationship which often bubbled to the surface in my presence. They never felt the need to put on for me.

I have witnessed more serious sibling rivalries, which seem to emanate from a secret, malicious envy or some fear of being outdone. But Sophie never begrudged her younger sister, whom she called *Doodle* or *Doo*, for the social prominence she had gained, or for her superior ability to entertain a crowd. In social situations, Sophie generally played a supporting role, and she truly admired Talley's notable conversational talents. But at home, there were constant domestic battles over tiny concerns—so petty I can't remember a single one of those issues now. In those conflicts, Sophie nearly always prevailed. Although seemingly strong-willed, Talley generally backed down in the face of determined opposition. Sophie knew how to get her way. She'd had a lifetime of experience and knew precisely which buttons to press to make her malleable sibling surrender to her will.

In February of 1985, my wife Donna and I drove Grandmom and Aunt Sophie up to Port St. Joe, Florida, so they could pay one last visit to my Great-Aunt Lala, who was Evans, Sr.'s only sister. Sophie, Donna, and I spent the night at the Port St. Joe Motel, a rather unimpressive lodging with noisy plastic coverings beneath the sheets on the lumpy mattresses. It was, however, preferable to being cramped together in Great-Aunt Lala's little trailer a few miles away where Grandmother was staying.

Sophie and I always shared the same spirit of Wanderlust, and in the morning she was eager to join my wife and me on a drive through the back roads to Panama City, Wewahitchka, and several obscurer destinations I'd found on my map. Before we left on our excursion, I thought it best to call my grandmother to report on our plans. When I got Talley on the phone, she said she wanted us to drop Sophie off at Lala's trailer.

"Grandmother would like to talk to you," I said, trying to hand the phone to Sophie. "She wants you to stay with her."

"That's too damn bad!" Sophie insisted, waiving the phone away. "I'm going to Panama City!" And she did!

My wife and I always had a great time with Aunt Sophie. She was one of the most cheerful people I have ever known. Although she sometimes described herself as an "old maid," her decision not to marry did not hinder her determined happiness.

One time she told me the tale of her only love. His name was Grover Cleveland Morgan. They dated for a time, and then he asked her to move out West with him—to someplace in California. She thought about it hard, she said, and struggled mightily with her decision.

"I couldn't leave Mother and move so far away," she told me. Tears welled up in her eyes. She said she never saw her boyfriend again.

Above all, Sophie was a traveler. She visited all but six states in the Union. Her biggest regret at the end of her life was that she would never live to see New England. At least one of her trips across the country was made by bus. One time on a cross-country trip, a man was sitting next to her. As the long hours drifted by, he fell asleep and his head dropped to her shoulder for part of the night.

"Mother, I slept with a man," she reported, when she returned home to Tampa.

"Sophie Louise!" her mother exclaimed. "I'm surprised at you!"

Then she laughed and told her mother about the innocent event on the bus.

One of Sophie's proudest days was when she was crowned queen and sat on a throne on the Maas Brothers float in Tampa's famous Gasparilla parade. In spite of her obesity—she was five feet tall and very rotund—Sophie beat out the more attractive employees and gained a glory she savored forever.

"I got the colored vote," she explained.

Everyone loved Miss Sophie. She was always kind, always accepting of everyone in face-to-face encounters. But discussions of creed were another matter. When it came to abstract social theory, she was trained to go by the book.

Sophie and Talley had difficulty coming to terms with changes in the harsh social order they had known for most of their lives, yet whenever they watched an African-American contestant on *Wheel of Fortune* or *Jeopardy*, they were always pulling for him or her to win. Talley told me one of the political differences she had with her husband, which caused her anguish when he was in politics, was that he favored eliminating segregation long before she could begin to accept a new way of looking at the world. One time she even told me she thought Evans was really a Yankee at heart, which in her old-fashioned lexicon was akin to calling him a devil-worshiper.

"You know his father was born in Ohio," she snapped, as if that trumped Evans' mother's deep roots in the South, not to mention his own birth in Florida—and his Southern accent. But that was just a passing flare of old-time Southern passion, which sparked when I treaded too deeply into subjects I knew better to leave alone. Was she channeling the spirit of her despised Grandpa McKewn? We are all made of contradictions. It's a good thing Talley didn't live long enough for my cousin Kathleen Garrett Roberts to track down Alonzo Crary's discharge papers. Evans' great-grandfather turned out to be a bugler blowing reveille for the North in Missouri's Union cavalry. "Aha—I knew it!" I can hear Talley say.

The thought of ever voting for a Republican made Sophie turn red in the face. She was a fierce Yellow Dog Democrat until sometime during the Reagan Revolution. When Strom Thurmond switched parties, I think Sophie began to realize that "Useless" S. Grant was no longer the spiritual leader of the party the South once went to war against. Thurmond was born in her home state the day before Sophie was born—before the Wright Brothers got their rickety plane off the ground for a moment on a beach in the other Carolina. Eventually, we could discuss the pros and cons of all the candidates without her busting a gasket.

In the summer of 1992 my wife and I spent a week with Sophie up at Talley's cabin in the Great Smoky Mountains, while my grandmother was away on a trip. Sophie's eyes were failing due to macular degeneration, and she could no longer get around on her legs very well. Nevertheless, she lost none of her optimism, and she loved to go on country drives with us as much as she always did. On the way to Cherokee, where we were taking her to one of her favorite buffet restaurants, she looked out with her dim peripheral vision at the flowers on the side of the road, and then she noticed a new cabin on the side of a hill.

"That's what I love about this drive," she remarked. "I'm always seeing something new that I've never seen before."

More than anything I would like to capture Sophie's childlike sense of awe and hold it fast for all of my days. If she ever felt glum for more than a moment, she hid it well. I visited her in the hospital after she had her gall bladder removed. She was moaning softly in pain as I entered the room.

"How are you doing, Sophie?" I asked.

"I'd have to die to feel better," she said, and she tried to laugh.

After she came home from that operation, she and I were sitting together at the dining room table in Talley's house. She told me she was supposed to stick with a new diet.

"The good part is," she said, "the doctor says I can eat all the lettuce I want!"

Then she stuck out her tongue and made a funny face. It wasn't too long before she was lapping up spoonfuls of gravy like she always had. Sophie loved country ham, and fried chicken, and biscuits, and anything with hog jowls in it.

Miss Sophie Louise McKewn

Sophie continued to tell Talley what she was and was not going to do. Sometimes the tension in the TV room could get pretty high. I always stayed out of the middle of their arguments. Usually they ended with Talley huffing, puffing, and surrendering in silence. Her only recourse was to hope for some future retreat into solitude. She would express her frustration to me sometimes as she followed me to the kitchen door when I exited her house.

"Honestly—I don't know what I'm going to do," my grandmother would whisper desperately. "She's driving me crazy!"

"You're going to miss her when she's gone," I'd say.

Sophie left us in December of 1994. About a year later, Talley said, "You always told me I'd miss her—and I do."

The last time I saw Aunt Sophie was two or three days before she died. Talley called the office and I raced over to her house with my cousin Mike. From the sound of the phone call, I was expecting to find Sophie gasping for her last breath.

"Hey there, love!" Sophie said to me as I entered her bedroom. She was lying still, and she barely opened her eyes. "Could you go get me a Lotto ticket?"

"Of course," I said, and I sat down beside her on the bed, while she dictated the six numbers she played every week. Her hands felt very cold. She didn't want me to pick up anything else for her—just a Lotto ticket. I drove over to a convenience store nearby on East Ocean Boulevard, and I brought back her ticket. I'm sorry to say that her numbers did not come in.

In those last few years alone, Talley became increasingly distraught. I'd still see that same happy performance when other company dropped in, but for me she always poured out her troubles. I made suggestions of ways of combating the blues, and always she asked me to tell her "Christopher stories." Those were tales I told about the latest mischief my youngest son had gotten into. He was a toddler then. She always loved hearing what he'd been up to.

"I knew that boy was going to be something special when I saw him in the hospital on the first day," Talley said. "He just lifted his head right up and looked around!"

On one of my visits, I told her about how Christopher came into my master bathroom while I was brushing my teeth getting ready for work that morning.

"If I made big mess, will I get big time-out?" the little redheaded 3-year-old asked.

"Well, did you make a big mess?"

"No," he insisted.

"Are you telling the truth?"

"No, I not telling the truth," he responded.

"Why not?"

"Because I not want big time-out!"

Afterwards Christopher showed me where he had torn up a Styrofoam block downstairs, spreading the little pieces everywhere. The incident was too funny to warrant punishment. Instead, he got away with agreeing not to make more messes like that without first gaining permission.

Those sorts of tales would turn that sparkly light back on in my grandmother's eyes before I left—but on my next visit I would find her troubled as before. This was a major role reversal. During much of my adolescence, she had been my counselor in so many difficult times when I found myself languishing in the doldrums.

In her mid-90s, Talley told me she had finally realized her mortality. I was surprised. For me, Death has always been lurking in a dark recess just down the block—and for as long as I can remember I have never thought I would tarry here in this sublunary realm for very long. So, I marveled at my grandmother's ability to make it for nine-and-a-half decades without realizing the woeful bell might soon be tolling for her.

When Talley was nearing death in July of 2002, I didn't want to let her go. She had been such an important fixture in my life for all of my 47 years. On top of that, she was my last living link to the distant history of my family and those faraway roots to which I felt myself anchored. I couldn't help but feel there were memories I had not captured. There were truths she had not told and things I still had failed to comprehend. On my last visit to her, I sat on her bed and held her hand. Her eyes were closed much of the time, but she was struggling against the effects of some strong sedative.

"Is there anything you haven't told me, Grandmother?" I asked.

"Ask me a question," she said.

Well, there were so many questions I still had revolving in my mind, but somehow it no longer seemed appropriate to dig deep enough to solve any more family mysteries. Instead of searching for new details, I thought it best to simply hearken back to old stories she had always told.

"Tell me about Orangeburg when you were a little girl," I said.

"We went there every summer," she said, dreamily.

"How did you get there?"

"On the train—we always rode on the train, except for that time we went up by car. That was quite a trip! My father got so mad. The car engine got so hot, the hood ornament melted. The first day we made it to White Springs."

She had always told me it was Live Oak before.

"We wanted to get water from the Suwannee River—for souvenirs, but the bridge was much too high. We tied strings to the bottles, but the strings weren't long enough."

"Where did you stay that first night? Was there a hotel?"

"I can't remember," she said, and for a moment she seemed to be falling back asleep.

"When we got to Orangeburg," she continued, "everyone came out to see us. We'd accomplished a great feat. I don't know how we ever found our way. We didn't have roads like today, and some of the rivers didn't have bridges."

As we arrived in Orangeburg once again, I decided to leave her to rest with her pleasant childhood memories.

Talley Crary on her 90th birthday.

"I just can't imagine a world that doesn't have you in it, Grandmother," I said, in parting.

She opened her eyes halfway and a tear rolled out.

"I'll always be with you," she said. "You just keep on being the same swell boy you've always been."

Talley squeezed my hand tightly, and I squeezed hers. And as we let go of one another's grasp, I realized we were saying our final goodbye. But I wonder—are there ever any real goodbyes for those few special people in our lives whom death can never take away? No, I don't really think there are. In a way, I feel like Talley and Sophie will always be waiting for another unplanned visit—just a little bit down the road.

Our Titanic History

There is a storm at the heart of Treasure Coast history—a raging whirl of crashing waves and howling winds. In a single night 300 years ago, Spain's entire fleet of treasure ships suddenly went down scattering untold millions of dollars' worth of silver and gold along our shores. After treasure hunters regularly began bringing up great caches of lost riches in the early 1960s, our region was dubbed the Treasure Coast. But the glitter of that shimmering nickname is only a half-told tale. The storm scattered people, too.

The drama of the 1715 treasure fleet disaster should have become as legendary as the sinking of the Titanic. But the people involved were all twice-doomed. First, they were caught up in one of the worst maritime catastrophes in history, and then their epic struggle was so overlooked it sank into oblivion. Swallowed by water, buried by sand, all traces of that dreadful event were wiped from the world's collective consciousness. For nearly two-and-a-half centuries, no one even remembered where the great disaster occurred. It was not until treasure hunters caught gold fever that archeologists and historians began to piece together clues. An outline of lost history reappeared.

Long, long ago there was a terrifying night when nearly 2,500 men, women, and children huddled together in the suffocating holds of 11 towering wooden ships. It was July 31, 1715, and the passengers had been rolling and tossing in the sea's increasing fury since the day before. A microcosm of Spanish culture of that era was traveling on those ships, including merchants, mariners, public officials, servants, and royalty. There was even an art collector among them, and a former governor of Florida.

These were people who had ruled the world. After all, God gave the Americas to Spain—or so Pope Alexander VI had decreed two centuries before. Ever since the early 1500s heavily-armed fleets of treasure ships had been transporting the silver of the Incas, and the gold of the Aztecs, and the glimmering treasures of the Mayans back across the ocean to Europe. Spain became addicted to its New World riches like a drug. The king and his favored subjects used them to buy luxuries made in manufacturing nations like Holland, England, France, and the German principalities. All of Europe shared in the elation, and wars were spawned to siphon off more profits. Even in peacetime, Spain's treasure ships needed to band together to fend off attacks her enemies made through state-sponsored terrorists, better known as privateers or pirates.

There were actually two flotillas of treasure ships making that ill-fated voyage in the summer of 1715. One squadron commanded by Captain General Don Antonio de Echeverz had picked up precious freight in South America. The other group led by Captain General Juan Esteban de Ubilla loaded up with treasure in Mexico. The primary cargo was silver, which is why the combined convoy is often referred to as the Plate Fleet (*Flota de la Plata*). *Plata* means *silver* in Spanish. But there was plenty of gold, too, and vanilla, chocolate, sassafras, and other sumptuous luxuries for the folks back home. They even carried crates of costly porcelain from China that had been shipped across the Pacific and carried over the deserts of Mexico on the backs of burros. After considerable delays, the two flotilla commanders finally made a rendezvous in Havana, where they filled up every remaining nook and cranny of their ships with passengers.

Even without the bad weather, it would have been an uncomfortable journey from Havana back to Spain. In the dank pantries below deck, provisions molded and grew stale quickly. Drinking water typically spoiled as weeks went by, especially when rats drowned in it. By the end of a transatlantic voyage, people usually had to hold their noses to swallow. Obviously, you needed a strong immune system just to make it through the meals. But a handful of upper class passengers could expect their supply of wine, brandy, and fresh meat would last through the trip. Animals were kept on board to slaughter for first-class dinners. The livestock added to the ripe smell in the cramped compartments most passengers had to share. But favorites of the king could book a small room up top with a window, where it was much easier to breathe.

The pageantry of coming and going was wonderfully colorful and exciting. Cheering crowds and firing cannon celebrated the grand departure of the Plate Fleet as it sailed out of Havana's harbor. It was a beautiful day when those 11 Spanish ships left together in full sail with banners flying. There was, as yet, no hint on the horizon that this would be the voyage of the damned. Oh, and there was one more ship tagging along. The *Grifón*. It was French. France and Spain had become allies again, so the *Grifón* was allowed to sail under the protection of all the many dozens of big Spanish guns lined up along multiple decks in each vessel.

Perhaps the highest-ranking nobleman on board those ships was Don Pedro de Colarte y Douvers. Although born in Flanders to a Flemish navigator, Colarte had worked his way up in influential Spanish circles, becoming one of the leading traders in the New World. He did very well for himself during the long, uneasy reign of the prior inbred king, Charles the Bewitched. Charles was a deformed and gruesome regent, who believed some wicked demon had cast a spell on him. He burned many alleged witches in an effort to cure his unfortunate birth defects.

Colarte, as one of the paranoid king's favored businessmen, had been elevated to the regal class in the 1690s. He was now known as the Marquis of Pedroso. Rich and royal, the Marquis was also a renowned art collector. One of his magnificent Murillo paintings, *The Heavenly and Earthly Trinities,* hangs in the National Gallery in London today.

When Charles the Bewitched died childless, the world's attention became focused on who would become the rightful king of Spain. The balance of power in Europe and North America depended upon the answer. Many died in what was called the War of Spanish Succession. The conflict impeded the regular flow of treasure back to Spain for more than a decade, until a peaceful settlement was finally reached. That's why the 1715 Plate Fleet was overloaded with extra silver and gold, much of which was being smuggled to avoid the royal tax.

During the recent war, the British had attempted to seize St. Augustine, but Florida's brave governor, José de Zuñiga y la Cerda, successfully fended off the siege from inside the walls of Castillo de San Marcos. Zuñiga and the entire local population crowded into that small fortress and outlasted a long attempt to starve them out. That selfsame governor was sailing with the Plate Fleet, too. Zuñiga, who was now 61, had since been promoted to the office of Governor of

Cartagena, the port city where South American treasure had been collected. He must have been born under a fortunate star, because once more he would look upon disaster from a place of safety. For some reason, he had chosen to ride back to Europe on the French ship, and the French commander was the only officer in the whole flotilla who was at liberty to think for himself.

They might all have been okay, if Captain General Echeverz had kept up the pace, but his six lumbering ships continuously fell behind as they sailed up Florida's coast. Captain General Ubilla slowed down repeatedly to let the laggards in the other squadron catch up. As a result, the fleet lingered a day too long in a region they should have hurried through. In the eyes of Spaniards, southern Florida was the *Terror Coast*. Passengers would likely have told ghost stories about the place, where savage natives were known in centuries past to have sacrificed castaways to their bloodthirsty gods. Few shipwreck survivors had lived to tell the tale of their visit. Perhaps they should have avoided sailing past the danger zone altogether, but they couldn't resist using the Gulf Stream as their water highway home. The current gave their bulky vessels a desirable boost.

Several days into the journey, the ships began to encounter a telltale roll on the otherwise pleasant sea. They rocked from side to side as they plodded northward. Cirrus clouds stretched out across the sky in the ominous shape of mares' tails. These were signs that mariners recognized as harbingers of nasty weather. A powerful disturbance was approaching from the east. As the hours passed, ocean swells grew larger and fringes of white caps appeared.

A wealthy ship owner named Miguel de Lima was sailing his boat, the *Urca*, in Captain General Ubilla's squadron. He first noticed the wind beginning to blow stronger as Ubilla's squadron sat waiting once again for Echeverz's heavily-laden vessels to catch up. They were near the treacherous region their destiny would one day give a name—the Treasure Coast. Ubilla should have lost no time in sailing northward beyond the reach of danger, but he was determined to keep the entire fleet together. In retrospect, he might have saved his own ships, if he had left the stragglers behind, but he wouldn't live to second-guess himself. Ubilla's squadron waited for lumbering Echeverz as the winds grew ever stronger.

When the ships regrouped, Ubilla ordered cannon shots fired to gain everyone's attention. He signaled his orders with flags. All vessels were commanded to face the wind and sail into the storm to reach for deeper waters. The fleet's leader was afraid to maintain his northbound course, because that would have meant tacking dangerously close to Florida's offshore reefs. Besides, he and his crews had weathered storms before.

One ship disobeyed and pulled away from the pack in time. It was the *Grifón*. The French commander, a man named D'aire, made full use of the wind and darted up the coast. Sailing away to safety, it must have been poignant in years that followed for Governor Zuñiga to remember looking back upon those 11 mighty ships in all their glory. He would have been among the last to witness those majestic floating fortresses gathering together to attack the storm, as dark clouds brought the night on early.

"The sun disappeared and the winds increased and increased in velocity coming from the east and east-northeast," Miguel de Lima wrote seven weeks later in a report dated October 19, 1715. "The seas became very great in size, the wind continued blowing us toward shore, pushing us into shallow water. Then the wind changed to a furious hurricane and the seas became of such great size, with huge waves."

The pitching and rolling continued relentlessly through the early morning hours of the 31st, and the ships were pushed miles apart from one another. As the storm became more damning, priests took confessions of seasick passengers who feared dying with unforgiven sins. All the while, ocean-hardened mariners on deck fought to press toward deeper waters. But the sails ripped, and the masts cracked off, and the rudders broke away. Mounding waves washed many seaman overboard before the battle with nature was lost.

As a last-ditch effort to stop the ships from reaching the crushing shallows, they dropped big anchors to claw against the sucking currents. The anchors would not hold. High up in the stern of one of those tall ships, the Marquis of Pedroso must have been bouncing off the walls of his private cabin as the hurricane tossed his rudderless ship like a toy. Crowds below rose and fell with each sloshing, mountainous wave. In the blackness of the night, their terror must have seemed a thousand times greater than if they had reached the dawn.

One by one the wooden fortresses crunched against jagged reefs, as waves thundered like waterfalls pounding down from on high. The sounds of the massive hulls splitting must have echoed horribly through the holds as blasts of saltwater rushed in to swallow people praying in the dark. Boats broke apart spilling people and treasure into the violent sea. Those who managed to find the surface to gasp for air would be pushed underwater again and again. In the darkness they could not have seen the shore, or judged how long they had to fight against the waves.

Admiral Don Francisco Salmón, second in command of the fleet, was on a ship that broke into three pieces, but it was so close to shore that the bow and the stern swept up to the beach. Most of the people inside those two fractured sections simply tumbled out into the landward fringe of the breakers, while those in the middle contended with the undertow that pulled them away from shore. Luckier still, Miguel de Lima's boat missed the reefs altogether and crashed into a shallow river inlet. Nearly everyone on his ship was spared. But the other nine ships went under much further from shore.

The number of casualties was staggering. According to first reports reaching a Boston newspaper several months later, 786 people drowned. Later computations set the death toll as high as a 1,000. The Marquis of Pedroso and Captain General Ubilla were among the dead. The grim light of dawn disclosed bodies rolling in the surf and washing up for more than 40 miles along the beaches from Stuart up to Sebastian and beyond.

By the time the hot sun rose, most survivors had made it onto the desolate barrier islands. Some had been too battered to continue breathing very long. Only a few of those still clinging to flotsam out at sea would find their way to the shore within the coming days. But getting to the beach was only the first stage in a long struggle to survive. The region was far removed from the civilized world, and the dog days of August were just about to begin.

"The heat of the sun was insufferable," Miguel de Lima wrote, "and the number of mosquitoes was probably greater than the plague of Egypt."

The stunned castaways congregated in several encampments on the beaches of what would one day become Indian River, St. Lucie, and Martin Counties. There were as many as 1,500. Admiral Salmón took charge of the settlement from his headquarters at the largest encampment, which was two miles south of present-day Sebastian Inlet. Wells were dug behind the dunes, where they found water that was fit enough to drink. Miguel de Lima was able to remove provisions from his battered boat before it sank altogether. The biscuits and other foods he rationed helped many castaways survive for the 31 days it took for the first relief ships to arrive with additional supplies. As for the hundreds of dead, they were given makeshift graves in the sand.

Fortunately, two small life boats with sails remained intact, and Admiral Salmón used them to send messengers to Havana and St. Augustine to ask the governors of Cuba and Florida for assistance. The most prominent castaways were allowed to sail away to civilization with Salmón's messengers. A few larcenous opportunists stole as much treasure as they could carry and walked 120 miles to St. Augustine, where they were arrested. The rest of the passengers sweltered and swatted bugs for a month, before the first rescue sloops arrived from Havana. Some had to wait much longer. Even after the rescue, the ordeal would continue for many.

"I have suffered such great losses from this disaster that I lack the funds to get back to my home or even to maintain myself in Havana," Miguel de Lima lamented. "However, I am happy that I still have my life and health."

Admiral Salmón's encampment near Sebastian Inlet continued to serve as headquarters for Spain's salvage operations for several years.

With the help of hired Native American divers, around half of the lost treasure was recovered and shipped back to Spain. But some of the treasure was lost all over again when several hundred pirates attacked the salvage encampment in 1716. The Spaniards found life in the area much too hostile and unpromising to consider establishing a permanent settlement.

After salvage operations ended, the encampment below Sebastian Inlet was abandoned to be covered by the sands of time—literally. The dunes along the coast remained untouched for hundreds of years, but now most of them have been claimed by housing subdivisions and condominiums of recent origin. A small stretch of seascape in the vicinity of Admiral Salmón's encampment has never been developed. It is part of Sebastian Inlet State Park, a perfect place to take a seaside stroll and witness what eternity has erased. Could there be a clearer illustration of the words of King Solomon? *There is no remembrance of men of old, and even those who are yet to come will not be remembered by those who follow.*

At the southernmost end of the state park you'll discover a hidden treasure: the McLarty Treasure Museum. If you blink you will miss it driving by, and even most longtime residents of the Treasure Coast probably don't realize it is there. The museum has been open since 1971. Inside, you will find many artifacts of the 1715 Plate Fleet disaster on display: ship's tackle, weaponry, pottery, porcelain, and dozens of pieces of eight. They are relics that still wash up in hurricanes from time to time. At the Mel Fisher Museum a few miles away in downtown Sebastian, you can also see plenty of gold—and touch it, too.

Musing upon museum collections of maritime relics and treasure, we can begin to piece together our story that is as big as the Titanic. Of course it must have gold, silver, and lots of jewels. But there will be broken hearts in distant harbors—lost dreams, lost hopes, lost graves, and a vanishing empire, too. We will have struggles with courage and cowardice, good and evil, but the triumph of the human spirit will prevail—that unstoppable will to keep on going and help one another survive no matter what life throws in our way. In the end we will discover our story is more than silver, more than gold, more than an endless striving to reach the future—this stirring drama of the Treasure Coast—and it came out of a storm.

McLarty Treasure Museum in Sebastian Inlet State Park.

The Majesty of Cattle Country

Bud Adams

Several miles past I-95 as you drive west on Orange Avenue the landscape is mostly sky, and our inconstant Florida skies are always so intriguing. But the wide celestial vistas feel so much more luxurious when dollops of hardwood hammock are added here and there. As you feast your eyes upon those islands of oaks and sabal palms—or cypress trees in the wetlands—you have to wonder how anyone ever undervalued the natural beauty of our state.

If you love hammocks, as well you should, you will love the astonishing panorama of Adams Ranch in western St. Lucie County. It feels like a never-ending gallery of Beanie Backus paintings, which is to say that Adams Ranch looks like every longtime Floridian's dream.

It has been aptly dubbed "the ranch of 10,000 hammocks."

The beauty of Adams Ranch is no accident. An artist of sorts, who understands the ways of nature, has been at work on the terrain for nearly seven decades. Since 1949, Alto Lee "Bud" Adams Jr. has lived in the same cypress house he built for his new bride, Dorothy "Dot" Snively, a former Cypress Gardens belle from Winter Haven. The young couple married the year after Bud began managing the family ranch. Nearly 66 years later, much about their house — so beautiful in its simplicity — still speaks of Florida in the olden days, including the home's absence of air conditioning in all but the bedrooms. Bud's love of his native state is tried and true, right down to the genuine swelter that comes with a summer day. Fern-clad oaks Bud planted over a half-century ago tower above the house. The blanket of shade they offer cools a back porch that looks out into a cavern of inviting greenery.

Bud was born on April 4, 1926—Easter Sunday—in Fort Pierce. He must have known early on that ranching was in his blood. His maternal grandfather, Silas Lee Williams, was a cattleman up in the panhandle, where Bud's father and mother were raised. Bud's father, Alto Adams Sr., was a Fort Pierce attorney who gained local fame taking on controversial cases. For instance, he represented family members of the Ashley Gang against lawmen who gunned their loved ones down. Alto Sr. enjoyed a great deal of success in the legal business, and it wasn't long before he looked for sideline ventures.

In 1935, Bud's father bought some horses and teamed up with Thad Carlton, another local lawyer, to invest in a herd of cattle. Thad was a member of the famous Carlton family, whose ranching roots in Florida reach back to the Second Seminole War in the early 1800s, if not beyond. At that time, western St. Lucie County, like the rest of Florida, was all open range. That meant you didn't have to own the land to use it for grazing cattle. Fencing wasn't required by law until 1949, so every cattleman and his cows were free to roam at will, just like the Seminoles, who still had chickees in the area.

Bud was a boy when the back country he loves first got into his soul. Although he lived in town growing up, the countryside captured his imagination. By the time he was 11, his father had purchased thousands of acres of open range for next to nothing from a man whose taxes were in arrears. Other boys only played cowboy, but Bud seized his opportunity to live the dream. Before he was a teenager, he was making cattle drives to the middle of the state. He witnessed the thrill of longhorn steers charging over the banks of the Kissimmee River, swimming with their big horns bobbing. Cowhands working for Lykes Brothers received his father's herd on the other side.

Most young cowboys don't grow up with a father who suddenly gets tapped to serve on Florida's Supreme Court. But when he was 13 years old, the heavy hand of history moved Bud more than 350 miles away to Tallahassee for the rest of his childhood. But happily, he still got to spend summers riding the range with Irlo Bronson, the legendary rancher-politician who sold his land to Walt Disney. No doubt you've noticed that the road to the Magic Kingdom is named the Irlo Bronson Highway. Well, Bud got to go on cattle hunts and cattle drives with Bronson, who would sleep on the ground around a campfire with all the cowboys who worked for him. Bronson, whom Bud refers to as "Florida's greatest cattleman," taught Bud much of what he knows about the illustrious heritage of ranching and its down-home, egalitarian ways.

Surprisingly, most Floridians don't recognize that Florida is cattle country. Always has been—always should be. Before there were orange groves, coconut palms, beach resorts and bulldozers, cattle roamed the pinelands and the swamps of our peninsula. Hollywood has always narrowed the scope of its imagination to cowboys of the West, which is probably why the world still overlooks the stature and long history of Florida's cowmen. The cattle industry is Florida's oldest industry. It has been here for literally hundreds of years. Ponce de León is thought to have abandoned Andalusian cattle on the Gulf Coast in 1521, and Spanish colonial Gov. Zuñiga introduced laws that sparked a cattle boom at the beginning of the 1700s. Even the Seminoles became famous for herding cattle.

As a young man enjoying the campfires of cattle hunts, Bud became steeped in the lore of renowned cattlemen like Jake Sumerlin, the legendary "King of the Crackers," whose word was his bond. Honor is the polestar of the Florida cowman, and honesty is strictly—and sometimes hotheadedly—enforced. Sumerlin's famous cattle drives to Punta Rassa, where he was paid in gold, made him one of Florida's wealthiest men in the 1800s. And yet the cattle baron set the standard of a noble, no-frills life in the saddle that so many cattlemen still admire.

By the end of high school in Tallahassee, the Second World War had drawn Bud away from early dreams of returning to ranching. The Navy gave him a battery of aptitude tests at Camp Blanding in the north-central part of the state. That's when he and the military realized he has the sort of mind that can wrap itself around the greatest complexities of science.

"The Navy sent me to Emory University," Adams told me, as he gave me a tour of his ranch. "And there I studied calculus and nuclear physics under a man who'd just come back from Chicago working with Oppenheimer (the "father of the atomic bomb"). I was completely educated in hydraulics, thermodynamics—the whole engineering mix. I couldn't have gotten a better education anywhere in the world. And then the war ended before I got my commission… But, you know, we use some of what I learned every day. We are governed by the laws of physics, whether it's the way the water will run, how the heat will be dispersed—or the air—and everything else."

After the war, Bud continued his education as a civilian at the University of Florida, where he graduated with a degree in Economics. When he was only 22, he had some powerful opportunities in front of him. His father was on his way to becoming chief justice of the Florida Supreme Court and would soon be giving up the bench to run for governor against Fort Pierce native Dan McCarty, Jr. Bud's mentor, Irlo Bronson, was a powerful member of the Florida House of Representatives and would one day lead the state's Senate. Ed Ball, who managed the DuPont Estate and practically ran Florida from behind the scenes, was a good family friend and neighbor in Tallahassee, so Bud had enough powerhouse connections to pave his road ahead with a tandem career in law and politics.

"But politics was never my cup of tea," Bud said, as he looked out across his land. "I told my father, 'I'd like to go home and run the ranch.' "

To understand the implications of that young man's decision, you need to consider that St. Lucie County's population was only a 15th of the size it is today. The Adams Ranch property was practically as remote and primitive as it had been in the 1800s, when the earliest English-speaking settlers arrived in Florida territory.

"When I came back here in 1948," Bud said, "Orange Avenue wasn't extended on out. It was still a grade, and a group of Indians lived a couple of miles away. I had no source of help here. I was running the ranch by myself. So, I would get the Seminole Indians— Sam Jones and some of his boys—to help me herd the cattle. They'd bring their horses here. They were expert cowboys."

When he married Dot, whom he described as "the best-looking woman at FSU," he offered her a choice between living in town in Fort Pierce, or moving many miles out west to the hinterlands. Dot, who shared her husband's pioneer spirit, made the more adventurous choice. "I told her, 'You'll be the first white woman to want to live that far out,' " Bud said with a chuckle.

Bud brought his scientific know-how to Florida's frontier. Although he had never studied genetics in college, he read a book on the subject. A professor gave it to him. "He said, 'Read this over, and if you don't understand it, read it again.' "

Gifted with a quick mind, Bud comprehended the concepts right away. He also grasped the intricacies of agriculture and its markets, too. At the outset of his ranching career, he realized that Florida cattlemen needed to up their game. Although Spanish cows had adapted well in Florida for centuries, they were comparatively small animals. They didn't produce the big tender cuts of beef that post-war, prosperous American consumers demanded. Most of the Northern and European breeds suffered significant ailments because of our semi-tropical climate. The Cuban market, once the focal point of regional sales, had become a thing of the past. The route to keeping the cattle industry viable in Florida meant Bud would need to create a new breed

185

altogether. He envisioned an animal that could tolerate the sweltering conditions of the swampy South and still grow beefy enough to meet market demands, so he began experimenting with cross-breeding.

"I made thousands of matings of Brahman and Hereford cattle," Bud wrote in his booklet, *The Old Florida*. "The ones that worked, I bred. The others I culled. Gradually the cream rose to the top and we had cattle that were heat tolerant, heavy weaning and pretty good beef-type cattle."

That's how Bud made Adams Ranch world-famous. In 1969, the USDA recognized he had, in fact, created a better kind of cow: the Braford. That was also the year that Bud chartered the International Braford Breeders, now known as the United Braford Breeders, to control the quality of the breed. By the 1990s, the ranch was conducting another composite breeding program that produced yet another breed: ABEEF cattle. Just like the Braford, ABEEF cattle can tolerate a hothouse environment and produce quality beef with high cutability.

Adams Ranch has been family-owned since the beginning. It is ranked as the 15th largest cow-calf ranch in the United States. A cow-calf operation is one where a rancher keeps a permanent herd of cattle to produce calves for sale after they are weaned and sufficiently matured in feed lots. The calves are further raised by the ranchers who purchase them. Besides the ranch in St. Lucie County, Adams Ranch has locations in central and North Florida, and in Georgia. But the spread in St. Lucie County will always be what Bud calls "the home ranch." Recently, the ranch underwent an amicable division between Bud's family and the family of his sister, Elaine Adams Harrison. In 2012, the Harrison family created a separate operation of their own known as 4H Ranch.

About 30 years ago, Bud turned the management over to his three sons: Mike, Lee and Robbie. Mike took over as president when Bud retired. Lee is in charge of the Madison County operations and Robbie oversees the ranch's citrus groves. One of Bud's granddaughters, LeeAnn Adams Simmons, is also an important part of the management, coordinating public policy and all the details having to
186

do with various governmental regulations and programs. Other family members take part, and nonfamily personnel are treated like family, too. Coincidentally, some of the nonfamily employees even have the same last name, like Buddy Adams, the ranch's manager. Most of the work in the field is done on horseback. Bud still rides over the ranch daily in his SUV, and he offers his assistance and wise counsel.

The pastures are never overgrazed, so the roots run deep. That helps the topsoil retain its fertility, so the grasses grow thick and beautiful. It is soothing to watch expansive green fields, as wide as a Civil War battlefield, ripple and toss in the wind. Bud often takes his camera along on rides through the ranch, just in case he spots a caracara or a red-shouldered hawk—or maybe a sly gray fox. His balanced wilderness makes room for nature's necessary predators. Bud has been an avid photographer since the age of 10, and longtime readers of *Indian River Magazine* will be familiar with his wildlife pictures, which for years have graced the last page.

"Man has the power to care for the land and the animals," he writes in *The Old Florida,* "or the power to destroy. A perfect world is one with a good balance of man, animals and the land. Our planning and preparation is not in years, it is in generations."

Bud has been busy keeping a lookout for future generations and what they will need to retain a healthy quality of life long after he is gone. Fortunately for Florida's remaining wildlife and for all of us, he and his family have kept their 18,000 acres on the Treasure Coast in a condition that sustains the vital ecosystem we all depend upon.

"The Adams Ranch conservation program lies at the heart of our business," Bud says in *The Old Florida.* "The hammocks of Adams Ranch are the longest tract of hammocks left in the Indian River District. We hope to see it preserved... At my age, I am concerned about how the land will look 50 to 100 years from now."

Bud's leadership in cattle breeding and conservation have gained plenty of recognition. He is a 1999 Florida Agriculture Hall of Fame inductee, and he and his ranch have won practically every award a ranch can win, including the 1997 National Cattlemen's Beef

Association's Cattle Business of the Century Award and the Florida Fish and Wildlife Conservation Commission's 2013 Landowner of the Year Award. But the general population needs to take notice, too. To keep ranching alive in Florida and all the vital conservation that goes with it, you need people who love the cowboy way of life. Such devotion may be increasingly tested as developers move inland in search of areas for expansion. That's why the state and federal governments need to get their acts together to adequately fund conservation easement programs and reform tax inheritance laws in ways that incentivize future generations of cattlemen to hold onto ranchlands that benefit us all environmentally.

Although cattle raising has existed since biblical days, going back to Abraham and Lot, it was not until the last century that scientists in the saddle like Bud Adams began studying Earth's adverse responses to careless cultivation practices. Bud has been at the forefront of a movement to restore a healthy balance of nature that makes room for all God's creatures and for agriculture, too. The substance of deeper value that must be preserved, the thing that counts as much as life itself, is the land, the earth, the living soil — and all those stunning islands of trees that enclose a rich variety of birds and animals. The land produces the food we need and holds the balance of nature all life depends upon. In the end, that balance can only be sustained if urban dwellers get on board. For that to happen, those of us who crowd together in cities and suburbia expanding on Florida's coasts should take a look at the world through Bud Adams' eyes—and feel the majesty of cattle country.

Rick Crary and Donna Choate (later Donna Crary) in the early 1980s

The night before last, I discovered a wonderful memoir by a young surgeon from South Carolina, who served in the Second Seminole War: Jacob Rhett Motte. His journal, *Journey into Wilderness*, appears in its entirety on the Internet. I read the latter half of his book, beginning with when Motte took part in creating the Army's palm-log fort in Fort Pierce on January 2, 1838.

My wife Donna sat with me in our library at home, while I read out loud. We were both intrigued by Motte's accounts of the region as it looked almost a century before the first big land boom. He described the Indian River as abounding with so many fish, it only took an hour to catch enough to feed the entire regiment.

On the morning of January 16th, his regiment left Fort Pierce on a campaign to attack a big Seminole encampment down on the Loxahatchee River near what was then known as Fort Jupiter. General Jesup decided to march down via the "famous and undefined Al-pa-ti-o-kee Swamp" which traversed the western region of what is now St.

Lucie and Martin Counties. A large section of that area is now preserved as Allapattah Flats.

"A watery region indeed!" Motte wrote. "Behind us arose the forest of pine, like a dark wall; while before and on either side of us, the scene presented to our view was one unbroken extent of water and morass like that of a boundless rice-field when inundated…Indeed, the whole country, since leaving Fort Pierce, had been one unbroken extent of water and morass…"

The soldiers could have marched southward on drier ground, but it was easier for them to slosh through shallow water than it was to do battle with thick palmettoes on low-lying ridges of sand. Saw-toothed edges of palmetto fronds tore at their trousers and scratched away the skin on their legs. The endless swamp, dotted with hardwood hammocks, was full of "more snakes, mosquitoes and other venomous 'critters' than one can shake a stick at"—but it was viewed as less inhospitable than the higher ground.

"As we threaded this maze of countless islets, studding the unbroken surface of water in loneliness and silence," Motte continued, "amid all the wild romance of nature—far secluded from the haunts of civilized man and marked only by the characteristics of wildest desolation…we felt the most intense admiration, and gazed with mingled emotion of delight and awe."

Motte's enchanting account gave me a glimpse of how enormous and how beautiful the wetlands of the Treasure Coast were before Florida was drained to make way for millions of dollars and people. I remember how much swampier it was here when I was young. The summer I was 16, I wielded a machete on one of Lee Brock's survey crews headed by Eric Holly.

I remember one particularly swampy job when we were surveying lands in an area where a large subdivision named Mariner Sands was later developed. All day long we stood knee-deep in water and neck-deep in mosquitoes. I saw firsthand that most of South Florida was made to be covered in water and wildflowers—at least during the rainy season.

When we got up yesterday morning, I was itching to catch a look at some of the region young Dr. Motte marched through. I was thinking of writing a story about his encounter with our area. Happily, my wife was up for another adventure.

"It's like old times," Donna said, and she was right.

We were driving west on Kanner Highway toward Lake Okeechobee. Intermittent drops of rain warned us that the sky would try again to flood the land, but our spirits were not dampened, nor was our resolve. A true sightseer will take vistas any way they come, as long as the tires can hold onto the road. It's what we did when we were dating. During those months when I lived in Jacksonville, nearly thirty-five years ago, and on all those weekends when I visited her during the four years before we got married, we took long drives, come rain or shine—or even ice one time.

There were always new back roads to find in northern Florida, or up in Georgia. When we would visit my mother Mary Ann Crary and my sister Robin Keller in Western Kentucky, we covered most of that state, too. We found different routes to get up there through Tennessee. One time we drove way out of the way, so we could ride up the Natchez Trace through Mississippi. Most of the winding roads through the mountains of North Carolina, where my grandmother owned a couple of summer cabins, became our old friends, too.

Even after we married, during all those years before our sons Ricky and Christopher were born, we took more road trips than I can count, especially during the years I was active doing committee work for the Florida Bar. We've been to every county seat in our big peninsula, except for one. Donna and I have racked up literally hundreds of thousands of miles together—most of them on back roads. I think I was born holding onto a steering wheel.

Donna was the only girl I ever dated, who never complained about my sightseeing explorations. I remember one of the girls before her once said—as she got in my old blue Volkswagen for a drive from Gainesville to Crescent Beach: "Here we go on another trip to nowhere." Well, I could tell right then and there she wasn't going to be *the one*. Neither were any of the other girls who were more interested in reaching destinations than enjoying endless journeys along the way. It never mattered how far I wanted to go, Donna would sit beside me and share the scenery. If I suddenly wanted to pull over on the shoulder and photograph her beside some pretty patch of black-eyed Susans, she would comply. Or she would pose amid the falling leaves.

Sometime early on, Donna decided to take up photography with me. If they had drones way back then, you could have spotted us in the middle of nowhere, each with a camera in hand, taking photographs of lovely scenery from all sorts of different angles. That's one of the ways you can discover hidden beauty in the world.

Yesterday was like that, only we were looking for beauty in our own home county of Martin. We have been living here together for over 30 years, but during that time we've mostly done our sightseeing someplace else. If you count the time before we married, or started dating—which hardly counts at all—I have spent over half a century in this favored place.

"When is the last time you saw Lake Okeechobee?" I asked.

"I can't remember," my wife said.

On the way there, we took a left turn into the Dupuis Reserve and drove several miles through the woods on the rough dirt road. When the rain tapered off, I rolled down the windows to get the full effect of being one with the pinelands and the breeze.

"This is so beautiful," Donna said, and several times during the afternoon she remarked about how very long it took her to appreciate the natural beauty of the real South Florida---the one beyond all the manicured lawns. Now she loves the rich and varied verdure of palmetto thickets, almost as much as I do--- and clumps of gnarly scrub oaks, horizons full of pines.

We saw the lake from atop the bridge at Port Mayaca. Donna expressed amazement at the vast expanse of calm, gray water. She wondered if it is blue on days when the sky is clear. And she asked some questions about the history of the lake, and I gave her a brief explanation of why Governor John Martin and others insisted it had to be diked. Then we drove out of our way to read an historic marker Donna spotted in front of a Southern mansion that used to be an old hotel.

Afterwards, we backtracked to Indiantown, before heading south to look for Motte's battleground in Jupiter. We made a stop at a convenience store. The short Central American Indian woman behind the counter was conversing in Spanish with the dark, diminutive man, who was visiting her. She spoke perfect English when I presented my purchases: bottled water for me; and a pack of peanut M&Ms for Donna. Other customers in the store were wearing hunting garb. Magazines at the counter were publications we'd never seen before, like *Mud Life* and *Hog Hunter*. So close to Stuart and Palm City, and yet Indiantown is in another world. That's the sort of minor revelation that makes a day-trip fun.

The heavens suddenly spilled out too much rain to visit the Loxahatchee Battlefield, but we drove south on 710 and then east on Indiantown Road anyway. I caught glimpses of extensive swamp I plan to revisit another time. I'll have to trudge through some of those acres myself, before I tackle writing about the Second Seminole War. I live by the maxim that if you feel the history for yourself, your reader will feel it, too. That's my theory, and I'm sticking with it.

I surprised my wife with a change of plans dictated by the continuing downpour. I knew she'd be thrilled if I drove her down to a couple of her favorite stores in Palm Beach Gardens. Any excuse to shop. While Donna sorted through racks of clothing and shelves of home accessories, I sat in the café of a nearby Barnes & Noble Bookstore and nursed a double espresso until the last drops were as cold as the air-conditioned temperature. Actually, I had time to read 10 whole chapters of Hemingway's posthumous book about Paris, *A Moveable Feast*. The book pulled me back toward distant days when I was living abroad in cheap hotels.

By the time we drove home on back roads, the rain had stopped and the sun was going down behind a gray soup bowl of clouds. I noted that smack dab in the middle of Jupiter Farms there is a sizeable cypress preserve. How wonderful! Urban sprawl is no longer eating up every inch of the overdeveloped regions beneath our more environmentally-conscious county.

We turned north on Pratt Whitney Road, where I saw places I've decided to return to photograph when the sunshine enhances the color—places like the Hungryland Wildlife Management Area.

"Ernest Lyons mentions the Hungryland from time to time in his writings," I told Donna.

We took a left on Bridge Road and wound our way back to Kanner Highway. By then we were out of the wilderness and driving through pasture lands. Donna began remarking once again how much more striking the natural world appears than all the made-up beauty in our urban world. She said she was game to take another daytrip around the big lake to Moore Haven sometime soon, so we can pick up that last county seat we've never visited before.

I looked over at my wife sitting beside me in the shotgun seat with her long blonde hair cascading into the fading sunlight that broke free from a dark cloud. There was an unmistakable spark of wonder in her soft blue eyes, as she looked out over the countryside sharing little observations. And I pondered how young and beautiful she still looks to me after all these years. Isn't that what our trips are all about--- finding indispensable moments of enchantment?

It was such a special day, the way all days should be. We both said so several times after we got back home---and later when we were falling asleep. And she was right, of course. Yesterday brought us back around to all those thousands of miles we traveled together before, as if this pleasant trip might never end. I never want it to end. Yes. She was so right. It was just like our old times.

Selected Bibliography

This list contains most of the books I found helpful to my purposes in preparing to write the stories in this collection. Newspapers and magazine articles I used have been specifically referenced within the stories themselves.

Akin, Edward N. *Flagler: Rockefeller Partner and Florida Baron.* Gainesville, FL. Univ. Press of Florida. 1991

Allen, Frederick Lewis. *The Big Change: America Transforms Itself 1900-1950.* New York. Harper & Brothers. 1952; *Only Yesterday: An Informal History of the 1920s.* New York. Harper & Row. 1931; *Since Yesterday: The Nineteen-Thirties in America.* New York. Harper & Brothers. 1940.

Ballinger, Kenneth. *Miami Millions: the dance of the dollars in the great Florida land boom of 1925.* Miami. The Franklin Press. 1936

Bishop, Jim. *The Murder Trial of Judge Peel.* New York. Simon & Schuster. 1962

Bramson, Seth. *Speedway to Sunshine: The Story of the Florida East Coast Railway.* Boston. Boston Mills Press. 2003

Brinkley, Douglas. *The Wilderness Warrior: Theodore Roosevelt and the Crusade for America.* New York. Harper Collins Publishers. 2009.

Brodsky, Alyn. *Grover Cleveland: A Study in Character.* NewYork. St. Martin's Press. 2000.

Brown, Cantor, Jr. *Ossian Bingley Hart*, Baton Rouge. Louisiana State Univ. Press. 1997

Burgess, Robert F. & Clausen, Carl J. *Gold, Galleons & Archaeology.* Indianapolis/New York. The Bobbs-Merrill Co. 1976.

Carter, Clarence E., editor. *The Territorial Papers of the United States, Vol. XXVI.* New York. AMS Press. 1973.

Chandler, David Leon. *Henry Flagler: the astonishing life and times of the visionary robber baron who founded Florida.* New York. Macmillan, 1986

Chapman, Frank M. *Autobiography of a Bird Lover.* New York. D. Appelton Century Co. 1933; *Bird Studies with a Camera.* New York. D. Appleton and Co. 1900; *Camps and Cruises of an Ornithologist.* New York. D. Appleton and Co. 1908.

Colburn, David R. & Scher, Richard K. *Florida's Gubernatorial Politics in the 20ᵗʰ Century.* Tallahassee. Florida State Univ. Press. 1980

Cutright, Paul R. *Theodore Roosevelt the Naturalist.* New York. Harper & Brothers. 1956.

Davis, Burke. *The Long Surrender.* New York. Random House. 1985.

Davis, William C. *Breckinridge: Statesman, Soldier, Symbol.* Lexington. Univ. Press of Kentucky. 2010.

Davis, Jefferson. *The Rise and Fall of the Confederate Government.* New York, D. Appleton and Co. 1881.

Díaz, Bernal. *The Conquest of New Spain.* Penguin Books. 1974

Dovell, J.E. *Florida: Historic, Dramatic, Contemporary, Vols. I & II.* New York, Lewis Historical Publishing Co. 1952.

Drane, Hank. *Historic Governors…Their Impact on the Sunshine State.* Ocala. A.H. Drane. 1994.

Dunn, Hampton. *Florida, A Pictorial History.* Norfolk. The Donning Co. 1988.

Fernald, Edward A. *Atlas of Florida.* Tallahassee. Florida State Univ. Press. 1981.

Flynt, Wayne. *Duncan Upshaw Fletcher: Dixie's Reluctant Progressive.* Tallahassee. Florida State Univ. Press. 1971; *Cracker Messiah: Governor Sidney J. Catts of Florida.* Baton Rouge. Louisiana State Univ. Press. 1977.

Fox, Charles D. *The Truth about Florida.* New York. Charles Bernard Corp. 1925.

Fuller, Walter P. *St. Petersburg and Its People.* St. Petersburg. Great Outdoors Publishing Co., 1972.

Galbraith, John Kenneth. *The Great Crash 1929.* Boston. Houghton Mifflin Co. 1961.

Graff, Henry F. *Grover Cleveland.* New York. Henry Holt & Co. 2002.

Hanna, A.J. *Flight into Oblivion.* Richmond. Johnson Publishing Co. 1938

Hellier, Walter R. *Indian River: Florida's Treasure Coast.* Coconut Grove. Hurricane House Publishers. 1965.

Henshall, James A. *Camping and Cruising in Florida.* Cincinnati. Robert Clarke & Co. 1884; *Book of the Black Bass.* Cincinnati. Robert Clarke & Co. 1881.

Hutchinson, Janet. *History of Martin County.* Stuart, FL. Historical Society of Martin County. 1975.

Hutter, Ernie. *The Chillingworth Murder Case.* Derby, CT. Monarch Books. 1963

Jahoda, Gloria. *The Other Florida.* New York. Scribner's Sons. 1967; *Florida: A Bicentennial History.* New York. W.W. Norton & Co. 1976.

Jeffers, H. Paul. *An Honest President: The Life and Presidencies of Grover Cleveland.* New York. Harper Perennial. 2002.

Johnston, Sidney P. *A History of Indian River County.* The Indian River County Historical Society. 2000

Lawson, Edward W. *The Discovery of Florida and Its Discoverer Juan Ponce de León.* St. Augustine. Edward W. Lawson. 1946.

Leish, Kenneth W., ed. *The American Heritage Pictorial History of the Presidents of the United States, Vols. 1 & 2.* American Heritage Publishing Co. 1968

Lloyd, Henry Demarest. *Wealth against Commonwealth.* New York. Harper and brothers. 1894.

Lowery, Woodbury. *The Spanish Settlements within the Present Limits of the United States.* New York. G.P Putnam's Sons. 1905.

Lyon, Eugene. *The Enterprise of Florida.* Gainesville. Univ Press of Fla. 1983.

Lyon, Eugene. *The Search for the Atocha.* Port Salerno. Florida Classics Library. 1985.

Lyons, Ernest. *My Florida.* New York. A.S. Barnes and Co. 1969; *The Last Cracker Barrel. New York. Newspaper Enterprise Assoc.*

Manley, Walter W. II and Brown, Canter Jr. *The Supreme Court of Florida.* Gainesville. Univ. Press of Fla. 2006

May, Ernest R. *The Progressive Era.* New York. Time Incorporated. 1964.

McDonell, Victoria H. *Rise of the "Businessman's Politician.": The 1924 Florida Gubernatorial Race.* Florida Historical Quarterly. (July 1973).

McElroy, Robert. *Grover Cleveland: The Man and the Statesman, Vol. II.* New York. Harper & Brothers. 1923

McGoun, William E. *Prehistoric Peoples of South Florida.* Tuscaloosa. Univ. of Alabama Press. 1993

Morris, Allen. *The Florida Handbook.* Tallahassee. The Peninsular Publishing Co. 1953; *The Florida Handbook 1981-1982.* Tallahassee. The Peninsular Publishing Co. 1981; *Florida Place Names.* Coral Gables. The Miami Press. 1974.

Morris, Lloyd. *Postscript to Yesterday: American Life and Thought 1896/1946.* New York. Harper & Row. 1947.

Motte, Jacob Rhett. *Journey into Wilderness.* Gainesville. Univ. of Florida Press. 1953.

Nolan, David. *Fifty Feet in Paradise: The Booming of Florida.* San Diego. Harcourt Brace Jovanovich Publishers. 1984.

Nevins, Allan. *Grover Cleveland: A Study in Courage.* New York. Dodd, Mead & Co. 1932.

Parry, J. H. *The Spanish Seaborne Empire.* New York. Alfred A. Knopf. 1981.

Peterson, Mendel. *The Funnel of Gold.* Boston. Little, Brown and Co. 1975.

Rights, Lucille Rieley. *A Portrait of St. Lucie County, Florida.* Fort Pierce, FL. St. Lucie Historical Society. 2006.

Roosevelt, Theodore. *An Autobiography.* New York. Charles Scribner's Sons. 1926.

Rowe, Anne E. *The Idea of Florida in the American Literary Imagination.* Gainesville, FL. Univ. Press of Florida. 1992.

Scott, George W.B. *Growing Up in Eden.* Knoxville, TN. Fountain City Publishing Co. 2004.

Seldes, Gilbert. *The Years of the Locust: America 1929-1932.* Boston. Little, Brown, and Co. 1933.

Selznick, Irene Mayer. *A Private View.* New York. Alfred A. Knopf. 1983.

Smiley, Nixon. *Yesterday's Florida.* Miami. E.A. Seemann Publishing. 1974.

Standiford, Les. *Last Train to Paradise.* New York. Crown Publishers. 2002.

Stockbridge, Frank P. & Perry, John H. *Florida in the Making.* Jacksonville. The de Bower Publishing Co., 1926.

Strong, William B. *The Sunshine Economy: An Economic History of Florida since the Civil War.* Gainesville, FL. Univ. Press of Florida. 2008.

Tarbell, Ida M. *The History of the Standard Oil Company.* Gloucester, MA. Peter Smith. 1904

Taylor, Deems. *A Pictorial History of the Movies.* New York. Simon and Schuster. 1943.

Tebeau, Charlton W. & Marina, William. *A History of Florida.* Coral Gables. Univ. of Miami Press. 1999.

Thomson, David. *Showman: The Life of David O. Selznick.* New York. Alfred A. Knopf. 1992..

Thurlow, Sandra Henderson. *Stuart on the St. Lucie.* Stuart, FL. Sewall's Point Co. 2001; *Historic Jensen and Eden on Florida's Indian River.* , FL. Sewall's Point Co. 2004.

Vickers, Raymond B. *Panic in Paradise.* Tuscaloosa. Univ. of Alabama Press, 1994.

Weisberger, Bernard A. *The Age of Steel and Steam.* New York. Time Incorporated. 1964; *Reaching for Empire.* New York. Time Incorporated. 1964.

Weigall, T. H. *Boom in Paradise.* New York. Alfred H. King. 1932.

Welch, Richard E., Jr. *The Presidencies of Grover Cleveland.* Lawrence, KS. Univ. of Kansas Press. 1988.

Westfahl, Arline. *Tales of Sebastian.* Sebastian River Area Historical Society. 1990.

Index